Finding the Road to Reason

Everything for a Reason Series Book 3

By: Julie Edgington

Dedicated to:

All my nieces, my nephew and my children.

Also to my furry friends Thelma and Chrismas.

Through it all you were with me and I survived because of you.

TABLE OF CONTENTS

AUTHOR'S NOTE

If you are new to the *Everything for a Reason* series, let me be the first to warmly welcome you. If you are continuing on along with me after our journey through Book 1, *Preacher's Li'l Secret,* and Book 2, *Love of an Angel,* I welcome you back again.

I write this book not just as a continuation of my story, but for all the souls out there that feel lost. Have you ever felt you live your life in a default mode, instead of knowing with absolute certainty that you are creating your own world, your own story, and that everything in your life happens for a reason? During my personal evolution I have spent years letting things happen *to me* instead of *because of me*. Even now, there are still moments where I am more human than spirit and my mind gets the best of me. Though the continuation of my story here deals with issues surrounding abuse, please know the experiences shared here are universal, even for those who have never experienced abuse. I believe my story holds meaning for all, at every stage of personal growth.

How is it that I am so certain? At some point in time we all have been a victim in one way or another. Being a victim doesn't necessarily mean we have been subjected to violence or abuse. Rather, we are a victim every time we don't take responsibility for what is happening, every time we can't find the lesson in our experiences, and every time we feel lost.

The word victim is a tricky sort of word and one that is often misunderstood because of its many connotations. For the purposes of learning from my story, hold tight to one implication of this word. That is, being a victim implies *that you are not in control.* And yet, I now know this is an illusion and I hope you will see this as well: *you have always been in control.* Many people simply need to learn how to be in control. That is, in each situation you must find your lesson, extract it from what you are going through and allow your soul to grow. This is the secret recipe to empowering yourself to have ownership of your life.

There was a time I was desperate and wished the world would just come to an end to ease my suffering. Perhaps you have felt this way at some point as well. As I said before in my book "Love of an Angel," the hard way out is when we fall into desperation. The world is mean to me and all those around me just want to cause me hurt and pain, we sometimes think. In hindsight, I see I was never a victim at all; all my hurt and all my pain had a purpose. Every single person that came into my life and all that happened occurred because I needed it to and because it was what I asked for. I gave every moment to myself, it was in my contract. It was all to make me strong and to make me into a person who could eventually understand enough to share my lessons with you.

Don't misunderstand me; I am not saying anyone should ever feel responsible for someone else's actions, especially actions which create victims. Also no one should ever feel they deserve to be treated badly, or abused, or that they asked for this treatment in any way. There really is no blame to be had. What I am saying is this: what is happening to you is yours and what you do with it is up to you. You gave it to yourself for a reason. Until you survive it, learn your lesson, grow, and then put it behind you, you will be stuck. As I wrote in Book One "Preacher's Li'l Secret," STUCK stands for See The UCK!

As you read this story, or any of my stories, please know I am never looking for pity or sadness, or to pass judgement on any of those who have wronged me. Instead, I share my stories because I hope you will take a new perspective from them and grow. Use the information I share to make your life better. Realize also that I know, and you should too, there is always going to be a story worse than yours. I am not saying my story is your story, but someone's is. It really isn't the story that matters anyways; it is the message behind it that is important. You can ask yourself why this story came into my life at this moment. When you ask, you will already know the answer.

If you are in an abusive relationship I urge you to seek help and know once you do, you will be okay. I know with every part of my soul how scary and hard it is to ask for help and how hard it is to be in an abusive relationship. But someday you will look back and remember your day, the day when you stood up and said "No more!" You will remember that day as the day when the rest of your life began. You are a special kind of person to have gone through what you have. You had you experiences and I am grateful to you because it means I and everyone else will never have to go through exactly what you did. Now you can contribute your experience to the whole and it will never have to be experienced in that exact way again. You had hard times and you did that for all of us. However you are done, you don't need to go through it anymore. You don't need to be any more special than what you already are. You are enough, just the way you are. You are more than enough. Please do whatever you need to do to get help.

If you read no further or take no additional learning from this book, please walk away with this lesson and my blessings for your every happiness: it is okay to ask for help.

CHAPTER 1

SEARCHING FOR A PLACE IN THE WORLD

"You're imperfect, and you're wired for struggle, but you are worthy of love and belonging." [Brene Brown]

You've heard it said before, as have I: some people just grow up too soon. I was such a person, perhaps you are as well. It doesn't matter what causes us to grow up too soon, when it happens it leaves a mark, almost like a fingerprint, on your soul. As I talked in previous books in this series and to recap only slightly, I didn't have a father and my mom passed away when I was young. I don't remember a time when I didn't feel much more grown up than my age would indicate I should.

There were other factors in my life long before Mom got sick and even before I realized what I was missing by not having a dad, things which made me something more than a child. Hopefully someday I will be able to address those factors in another book, but for now I will continue with my story.

At the age of eleven my mother passed away, as you may know from reading my second book, *Love of an Angel*. I was a child left alone in this world with no parents and surrounded by an abundance of narcissistic adults. I don't know which was more difficult when she passed away, being left alone to take care of myself or being left alone with the empty feeling of not having anyone to care for (I had been a primary caregiver for my mom, as a child). I had become accustomed to having someone to always look after and take care of, but I was stripped of that when Mom passed away, and I know that played into what happened next in my life.

I went to live with my oldest sister Deb and her husband Curt. Deb and I were not getting along well at all, to summarize briefly the story I have told in *Love of an Angel*. Before long, my second oldest sister Cindy agreed I could come stay with her and, not surprisingly, Deb seemed only too eager to sign over custody. I have no doubt she was as happy to get rid of me as I was to leave.

As a young girl who had just lost her mother, I have to admit it felt like yet another loss to be so easily disregarded, but at the same time I was happy to be free. Growing up, Cindy and Deb had taken sibling rivalry to new heights and I knew that by leaving Deb's home, Cindy would be sure I never saw either Deb or Curt again. As I left Deb's home, I thought it was the best thing that happened to me in a long time. Little did I know my life was about to get much worse.

I had lost quite a bit of weight after my mom passed away, due in part to grief and stress and also due to Deb who had metered and rationed and chosen my food during my time in her home. It was a healthy change for me in a way as I had become a heavier child than was probably healthy for my age. In a new environment, it didn't take long for me to regain the weight I had lost. I was heavy again. Sure, I was disappointed in myself, but at the same time I didn't care enough to watch what I was eating. I had spent most of my life overweight and it felt natural to me somehow. Around that time, I also began to suffer horribly with migraine headaches. Though I would complain, no one could understand the pain I was in. I learned to eat Ibuprofen like it was candy by the time I was twelve.

I quickly learned to be someone who survived without guidance or parents. I lived with adults, family even, but my sister was pregnant with her first child and was struggling with life in her own way. She simply didn't have the capacity to nurture me. Her husband wasn't much help either and was very abusive towards Cindy. Cindy and I both grew up watching as Mom endured abuse and sadly, for both of us, though abuse was nothing new in our lives, it was still a trigger of deep depression.

And yet, there were some good points to living with Cindy, it wasn't all bad. For example, I was able to see my best friend Mendy again, whom Deb had prevented me from seeing. I had missed my good friend and her family so much. Everything started to feel a little more normal to me. I tried to spend as much time at Mendy's house as I could because being there felt like I was closer to home. Mendy's family had felt like my own during the tumultuous time of my mom's illness and death, and I had missed that. With Mendy's family, I was more comfortable and happy than I had felt in a long time.

Unfortunately, after a short time, I spent less and less of my time at Mendy's house once my sister had her baby, my niece. Instead I would stay home and babysit to help out Cindy. I loved my niece and felt like taking care of her gave me a purpose again. Plus, I got paid in cigarettes and since I was smoking by that time, I thought it was a good deal. There were other privileges extended to me for my help with my niece, too. I was allowed to have anyone spend the night, even if it was a boy. I think about this "privilege" now and it blows my mind. I had just turned thirteen and was allowed to have boys spend the night? Of course I didn't act or feel like I was just thirteen, and definitely wasn't treated that way by anyone.

Cindy and I fought a lot, just as we had done when Mom was alive. It felt like Mom had gone on a long trip and Cindy was left in charge. We were in a similar power struggle daily with me living with Cindy, only this time she was not just my older sister but also my guardian, meaning I had to listen to her and couldn't simply stomp and fume until Mom got home. So in the beginning, I was happy when she left me to babysit because it meant she was gone from the house and I was in charge, not her. But this was only a temporary reprieve. When I was around Cindy, I consistently felt I was more of an adult than she was, so it was very hard to listen to her. And most of the time listening really only meant doing what she said when she told me to clean up the house, clean up everyone else's messes, and being told how stupid I was. At first I knew I wasn't stupid, but after a while, even I began to believe it.

Cindy was young then and she was my sister. She was someone I had spent my whole life fighting with, tattling on, and pestering. When I lived with her, I began to see her in a new way. Most notably, I watched as she became an alcoholic. As I began to grow up, she stayed the same or even worse. In many ways, I became an adult while she reverted to being a teenager again. All she wanted to do was party and do anything that required her to be away from home. Seeing my sister act like this made me unknowingly become the opposite of what she was, out of spite and to be contrary in any way possible. This is the kind of relationship we had.

Around the time I was fourteen, I saw a little hope that Cindy could be moving on from her life of partying and becoming an adult when she became pregnant with my nephew. She settled down a lot then and didn't drink or go out much anymore. I was glad for her in a way, but at the same time it made my life more difficult since she was around the house more often and we didn't have as much time away from each other anymore. She became even meaner towards me. I felt as if everything I did was wrong. I tried hard not to fight with her or upset her because she was pregnant, but there were times when no matter what I did it wasn't enough. She alternated between bitter about being stuck at home with kids, and being somewhat sisterly towards me. I never knew what to expect, or which Cindy I would find waiting for me at home.

After my nephew was born, Cindy got a job. I think work became her escape and soon she was not around the house much at all. It was almost better this way. If she wasn't home, it meant she was getting abused by her husband and it meant she wasn't having to deal with me as much. At the same time, I began to feel even more stuck. I was stuck knowing life sucked. I couldn't even count on tomorrow. I knew tomorrow would bring more misery, more sadness and most times, I wished tomorrow would go away.

The one thing I could rely on that I knew was the same day after day was that I would be in the house taking care of my niece and my nephew. I loved them dearly, but instead of being their aunt I was their fulltime care giver. It's true, you should be careful what you ask for. When I was younger, even before Mom passed away, all I wanted to do was babysit. I even took babysitting classes to learn how in hopes someone would hire me. I just loved little babies and how cute they are, and I guess I got my wish finally.

My only escape from my home life was school, which really wasn't much of an escape since school had become nothing more than a place where kids got together to judge one another. I went from being the nerd to a mean bad ass. Kids who had once picked on me began to fear me and I became known as a person who would do anything I had to regardless the consequences if it meant I got my point across. My point was simple, leave me alone. Everyone's problems seemed so meaningless.

I would listen as kids complained about their parents and it felt like nails on a chalk board. Anytime someone would complain, I would get away from it as fast as I could. I wanted to scream at them, but I knew they wouldn't understand how small and insignificant their problems were. I would go volunteer with special needs kids in our school at lunchtime just to make myself feel not so empty inside. I didn't view the special needs kids as less than myself, rather those kids were more my peers than the crowd of "normal" kids I'd left behind in the lunchroom. At least they knew there was more to this world than how high you could rat your hair or what your clothes looked like;

they had real problems, just like I did.

Although I had friends, I still felt alone. As each day passed, I felt myself getting further away from who I had been. I had progressed because of life's hard knocks from a quiet, nice, little girl with a mom to a teenage rebel with a quickly-deteriorating home life. I didn't want to live with Cindy and I knew I didn't want to live with Deb, but there weren't many other options. And then, one day before school, my friend, Mary, and I started talking and came up with a master plan. Her home life wasn't the best either, and together we decided we should run away. Lucky for us, although it was fall, it wasn't winter yet (Iowa winters are brutal). Our smart idea was to hitchhike our way to someplace warm before winter came.

Our junior high school was across the street from some cornfields. In Iowa when you run away you go where no one can see you, into the corn fields. Most people probably would have felt trapped by the seven or eight foot corn stalks, but not me. I liked being where no one could see me and where I controlled if I left or if I stayed. I think it is funny that now I live on a small acreage surrounded by corn fields.

Towards the end of the day I started to miss my niece and nephew and the thought of them not being taken care of plagued me horribly. If I really had wanted to, I am sure I could have been long gone that day, never to have been found again. My love for them kept me from running away though, and probably is the reason why Mary and I got caught. But in that short time as a runaway, I had a taste of freedom. I wasn't just free that day from everyone else's control, this was a special kind of freedom. It was a freedom of choice and a freedom of beliefs. I was free from all the hurt and pain. Nothing mattered, so long as no one could find me.

When I stood in the corn field that day for the first time ever, my life was a blank slate. I was free from all my thoughts, my feelings, and the experiences that had shaped me. It was as if I was invisible to the world, surrounded by tall guardian angels in the shape of cornstalks that could not hurt or judge me. That idea of freedom is what kept me going. I just knew someday I would be really free. For right now I was back to being a prisoner, but there was even freedom in making that choice. I chose to go back, no one forced me. Sometimes freedom is getting to choose your prison cell.

So, I went back to my life and the freeing feelings of freedom dissipated. I was miserable from head to toe, spirit to soul. I was sad and depressingly lonely. It is true, we do attract to us how we are feeling inside. I was about to attract someone who was as miserable as I was. Yet there was one difference between him and me. That is, he enjoyed being miserable. Even worse, he loved to make other people miserable, but had no reason at all for it except the sheer joy it brought him.

I was almost 15 when I met Larry. It must have been meant to be. I wasn't allowed away from my babysitting duties much, but for some reason the day I met him I was free to find my new prison. My new Alcatraz was disguised as a cute older boy with a car. I was attracted to him even though I knew little about him. My subconscious knew exactly who he was. He fit into my beliefs of how a man should act and treat a woman.

Before I knew it, Larry and I were always together. At least with him there, I wasn't left alone all the time with the kids anymore. He had a car most of the time and he could take the kids and me places so we weren't stuck in the house. Of course this was at Larry's discretion and happened when he decided he wanted to come to our rescue.

Cindy liked having Larry around so he could stay with me and I wouldn't complain as much. I had a grown up relationship to match the adult in me. The kid in me, even the teenager, had long gone and seemed nothing more than something which had happened in another life time. Even though I felt all grown up I wasn't ever in control of what happened to me. I lived life on default waiting for someone else to dictate what was next.

Although I had Larry there, the comfort I found in having him around was short lived. He would get very obsessed over the thought of me talking to other boys at school. No matter how much I tried to convince him, my word was nothing to him. He often would pick me up after school and would question me about anyone who was even standing by me, even if I didn't know them. He made me feel bad and I had not ever done anything to make him think I would be unfaithful.

The fear of being alone all the time again kept me from telling him to buzz off. Even if I did, I don't think he would have. He knew I didn't like being alone and would use it against me. He had not been physically abusive with me and I thought because of that, he was good. But, if I said something he didn't like or if he thought I had talked to another boy at school, he would punish me by not coming around when he knew I would be all alone babysitting.

Despite all the problems it caused, I still liked being at school. It was at least away from the house and responsibilities of everything being enslaved meant. School was the one place I could go where I could pretend to be a little normal. It was all I had, until one day I heard Larry and Cindy talking at the dining room table. Something quickly stopped me before I could continue on and I began to listen very carefully.

I felt all was lost as I heard my own sister and my boyfriend combining forces and uniting as one dictatorship and planning the takeover. The wheels of my world were in slow motion, each word spreading like a virus through my system. What I was hearing was their discussion of my future and the main topic was me dropping out of school. I listened as they fed off each other's ideas about how great it would be.

Larry never came out and said that he wanted me to stay home because he didn't want me around other guys, but it was implied. I don't think he wanted me around other people in general. I knew Cindy's objective was a personal slave/ babysitter. Knowing I wasn't going to have a choice, I took a deep breath and walked into the room acting as if I had not heard anything.

Cindy didn't even ask me how I felt about dropping out or if I wanted too, it just happened. I didn't say much about being forced to drop out. Throughout my whole life, I never really opposed what Cindy said, she had a way with words to make you feel stupid and about an inch tall. With no one around to make me feel better about myself, I knew I couldn't afford to protest.

If Cindy wasn't at work, she was out drinking. Without school as my escape the days started to run into each other. I would have my moments when I would get to a breaking point and tell her how I felt. It would always just start a fight, but I would pray for her to realize what she was doing to us. Her husband didn't care about the kids or me either. Even if he was there, I was still expected to do everything for the kids. One time I asked him why he couldn't change a diaper and he said, "Why do I need to when I have you here to do it for me?"

My sister would get angry when her children wanted me instead of her when she was around. My nephew, of his own free will, even started calling me mama. I loved them so much and they kept me getting up in the morning and they were the reason I cried myself to sleep at night. I didn't cry because I didn't want to be there with them; I cried because I knew if I left them we would miss each other. I knew if I left them, they wouldn't be taken care of. I truly felt trapped by my love for my niece and nephew and committed to protecting them from their parents.

Since Larry was around a lot and allowed to spend the night, it was just a short time before I became pregnant. My new delicate condition didn't matter to anyone and became more of a nightmare than anything. Not only did I have the responsibility of taking care of my niece and nephew, I was constantly sick and tired. The sickness never went away. The only time I felt relief was when I was sleeping, which despite being exhausted, I didn't do very well.

I prayed night after night that I would wake up the next day and there would be a change. I would pray to Mom, God and anyone else I thought would listen. I would day dream about what my friends might be doing in school. I just wanted to be normal like everyone else with a mom, a dad, a life, and a future. I wanted to have school work and get ready for prom and think about which college I would be going to. I wanted to hang out with friends on the weekends and have fun. I just keep hoping and praying day after day.

Despite my hopes, I slipped deeper and deeper into depression. My pregnancy kept me going because I knew I would love my baby. I knew I would finally belong to someone in this world again. I wasn't even scared about having a baby like most teenage parents, I imagine, are. Maybe it was my naive nature or maybe I was just happy to have someone who would love me. I knew I would be a good mom and I already had plenty of practice taking care of babies. I continued my prayers of begging for help and hoping tomorrow would bring me something good for a change. I never gave up hope.

CHAPTER 2

LESSONS ON HOPE

*"Hope is the thing with feathers that perches in the soul – and sings
the tunes without the words – and never stops at all."*
[Emily Dickinson]

Hope in the face of adversity and, for some, the most extreme of challenges, whether that be physical, emotional or spiritual, is an enduring theme of human existence. And it's a difficult concept for many. For some, hope abounds and is a cornerstone of a person's outlook on life, while for others, it seems elusive, something we wish we had more of and yet just can't seem to find. I learned a lot about hope during this transitional time in my life, from being a child myself – even though I was a mature one – to having a child of my own. And as I said at the end of this chapter, despite all the odds, I never lost hope. Why? How? What advice can I share with others in similar situations who are perhaps struggling to find and latch on to hope?

Many times I have asked myself why I wanted to keep hope, especially because there were times when it felt that hope simply could never be sufficient for what I was dealing with. Why does anyone do anything we do to keep surviving? The suffering and the agony at that time in my life was intense, and no amount of happiness I had in terms of looking forward to being a mother, could have eclipsed it. Every day, day after day, the pain of being stuck and lost grew stronger. Without even realizing it myself, I gravitated towards anything that would keep me going. For example, I clung to ideas of seeing my niece and nephew all grown up, and ideas of having the love of my own children someday. I moved forward in life because I hung onto the idea of my mother being proud of who I could become and the person I wanted to be when I was somehow, one day, free of my fears.

Hope comes from unlikely sources

I even gravitated towards situations that would, albeit painfully at times, remind me that I was still alive; I gravitated towards situations that would remind me that I wasn't hopeless and lost. There was a time just like this when, against my better judgement, I gravitated towards a confrontation with Cindy. I stood up to her one night when she was drunk, and she attacked me for it. Even though I knew better then to talk back to her when she was drunk, I could not have avoided this confrontation if I had tried. I needed to not feel helpless and, in this instance also, my mouth has a mind of its own and it called the shots that night.

She was furious and took out all her frustrations on me. First she began whaling on me with her hands; then she grabbed a table leg from a wobbly plastic night stand that stood next to my bed. I didn't even fight back; all I could do was lay on my stomach with my hands over my head, wishing she would stop. I didn't care what happened to me, I just didn't want her to hurt my baby.

Cindy's husband must have been alerted by all the commotion because he rushed in and stopped her by punching her in the nose as hard as he could. I looked up to see why she had stopped hitting me just in time to see blood splattered all over the walls and my sister holding her hand over her nose. The fact that my own sister didn't want me in our home anymore but someone, even if it was an abuser, thought my life was good enough to save, kept me going that night. After that, I latched on to the smallest shred of hope: I wanted to exist just because I knew if someone like her could belong in this world, I deserved a spot here too.

Hope sometimes looks like resilience

We are always striving for things we don't have or others don't want us to have. I discovered that this striving is an unlikely source of hope. For me, the idea of giving my daughter a normal life, something I could never have, became something that kept me going. The night I was beaten up by my drunk sister was the night I found a tiny sliver of hope in an unlikely place. What followed, was equally surprising and even more powerful. That is, I discovered that in striving for things we don't have, meaningful things, we uncover resilience. That night I discovered that I am resilient, and that I was stronger than I ever knew I could be.

The strength I found was in observing the control I had over my actions, how I used my inner strength to *not* fight back, which is a strange paradox. I had one mission that night, which was to protect my baby no matter what happened to me physically.

Hope is part of our nature

I have found through my experience that the question is less about how to find hope and how to press on in the face of adversity, and more about why we ever doubt that we have hope at all. The presence of hope deep within is more natural and a bigger part of our being than most of us ever realize. We are humans, yes, but humans have innate animal instincts.

One of those instincts is survival. Survival instinct is the number one reason we keep going. As animals we have some basic needs. One of those needs is to be loved, or at least liked, because if we are then that means we are more likely to survive. If we survive, we can carry on our DNA into future generations. Animals don't often understand their instincts (e.g., *why* there is a drive to be liked and carry our DNA to future generations), but it is a strong drive that keeps us going just the same. As long as we have a survival instinct, hope will be rising up to keep us fighting for survival.

Our survival instinct is not just for passing along our DNA to future generations. It also has a lot to do with the human aspect of our existence, which is learning our lessons. Recall from previous discussions in this series that humans write the bad things and the difficult things, which teach us our biggest lessons, into the contracts we have created before we come to this earth. We use our animal instincts to keep us surviving the bad things so we can last long enough to learn our lessons. I needed to go through what I did to make me who I needed to be, but I also gave myself something to help me move forward, in my contract. My baby was my light in all the darkness, the very tool written into my contract to help me through the hard times while I learned my lesson. And, though I couldn't have known this at the time, my baby also gave me something by which to measure my happiness against someday.

Depression still sneaks in

Even when you recognize that there is still a glimmer of hope, depression still sneaks in. In these times, every little thing that is not going well seems amplified, while the good things, the positive things, are muted and monotone. The accompanying sadness seems so final and maddening.

My personal experience with depression was that it left me angry, cold, but able to put up a good front to those who didn't know me well, and I learned to hide away from those who did know me. The only people I felt true love for were my niece and my nephew and my unborn baby. In hindsight, I know the truth in these words: it doesn't matter what caused you to be in this state of mind, but it does matter that you find your way out of it. Also, finding your way out of depression doesn't mean it will never haunt you again.

To this day I fight the depression demon. It nips at my ankles, trying to grab hold and drag me back to the darkness and emptiness I once knew. When this happens, I know now of a few ways to combat it. I keep it away by looking it in the face and confronting it. It doesn't always work, but I never stay in the emptiness long. Another thing that works for me and might work for you as well is that I pull myself up and focus on the real reason why I am here. For me, I recognize that it is my responsibility to share my words and knowledge with others. This is for the help of others, but it also helps me. In fact, it keeps me sane. I have learned through depression that serving others is a powerful way to fight depression and keep happiness in my life. When you are serving others, you are serving yourself because every one of us is part of the whole. If you find even one person to make happy, it will radiate through you.

My pregnancy

My pregnancy seemed to be progressing in slow motion, as if this time in my life would never come to an end. Everything moves slowly when you are a teenager, especially the exciting events. As much as it was exciting to be having a baby, I defiantly was not enjoying this special time in my life. Larry treated me like garbage and wouldn't keep a job, so there was constant wondering and worrying about where the money was going to come from to buy the things my baby needed. I would have never been allowed to have a real job. A job would have meant I was around other people Larry would not have liked that. It also would have meant I would not have been there to watch the kids for my sister. If I wasn't worried about Larry, I was dealing with being very sick. I hadn't been able to keep much down and at five months along I was hospitalized for dehydration. I continued to pray for relief and one day it finally came!

Around the same time I was hospitalized, a law passed in the state of Iowa which was the answer to my prayers. The new law raised the legal age to drop out to sixteen, meaning I was not eligible to be a high school dropout. For the first time in a long time, life felt better. I felt like God wrote that law just for me. All my hoping and prayers paid off and I was looking forward to getting back something that was so precious to me: an opportunity to leave the house and learn. They seem like simple things, but to me they were freedoms I had been denied for a long time and I appreciated them more for not having had them.

My sister found a way around the new law, but not completely. The alternative high school I went to offered half days. I was only allowed to go to school from 7:45 A.M. to 11:30 A.M., but back then I was grateful for it. Those were the best hours of my day and I looked forward to them. I started making friends again at school and learning gave back much of the self-confidence I had lost; being in a school environment again reminded me that I wasn't stupid, as I had been told to believe about myself at home. Being pregnant made it difficult for me physically and there were mornings when I had to get out of bed and get up even though I was tired and sick, but I pushed myself to do it anyway because generally I looked forward to school. And then there were days when I wished I hadn't gone to school.

I didn't mind being pregnant and in school, what I did mind was girls coming up and telling me they saw my boyfriend at parties and he was with other girls. I didn't believe them at the time, but it was probably true. One girl in particular made it her duty to taunt me almost on a daily basis. She had been hanging around Larry and he had been bad-mouthing me. Since Larry had gotten into the habit of going days and sometimes even a couple weeks without seeing me, she made it a point to tell me about the time she spent with him. When he did come around it was mostly to harass me about other guys he thought I was talking to at school. Sometimes I wished he would just go away and never contact me again. Then again, he was the only thing outside of school I had at the time to keep me from going crazy.

I didn't talk to Mendy and Mary much anymore. I saw them now and again, but they were busy being teenagers while I was stuck at home playing homemaker for my sister. Looking back now I can analyze my fears and come to some conclusions as to why I stayed in that situation for so long, but at the time I felt trapped and helpless. I was only 15 years old and having been conditioned my whole life to be a victim, I was living the reflection of what was in my mind.

This is what I call *living on default*. You live thinking you do not have a choice. You do have a choice though, you choose your resonance. You get to choose your thoughts and that is what creates your vibration. *No one* can ever choose your thoughts for you. This is an absolute truth and it will get you through your situation, no matter how bad it is. Whatever situation you are in is, abusive or not, the situation you have chosen for yourself because you aren't ready for anything else yet. Now that you are reading this, are you accepting these words as a wake-up call, realizing that *you are responsible* and you are *in control* of your situation?

I think back to myself in your situation, struggling to find answers and a way out, and I put myself in your shoes and wonder, if someone had told me back then at fifteen about the law of attraction, would I have been able to see it for myself? Would I have believed that I was responsible for my situation because of the thoughts I chose? I tend to think not, and that is where I hope you will be smarter than I was back then. For one thing, I was fifteen and believed that I knew it all, which is typical for this age. No one could tell me anything, it was just who I was back then. And yet, even this stubbornness came in handy and ultimately, it enabled me to learn one of my most important lessons. That is, I had to learn to stand up for myself and for what I knew I wanted and needed in my life.

As my due date grew closer my teachers began pressuring me to give up my baby for adoption. One concerned teacher set up a meeting with a woman who had given her baby up for adoption when she was my age, I suppose to help me gain some perspective on how productive this choice could be. I had gone to school that day, and I was about seven months pregnant at the time. The concerned teacher asked me to go into one of the class rooms that were empty. He told me I should at least hear what the lady had to say about giving her baby up. I told him I didn't want to give my baby up and I didn't want to listen to what the woman had to say. Somehow I ended up in the chair and in that room by myself. I was fuming with anger; if I was a cartoon character, smoke and fire would have been shooting out of my ears! I felt betrayed by the teachers who had not even cared enough to find out what my life was about or what I wanted for myself.

There was one teacher who didn't try to pressure me and who did take the time to know who I was and what I was going through. His name was Mr. Boaz. He cared for all his students equally and knew each one of us with his heart. Instead of trying to pressure me to give up my baby, he offered a place for me to come and live with my baby. He and his wife were prepared to take me in and help me while I finished school. It felt so nice to have him offer, but I turned down his offer. It was strange to me that someone cared so much about me. I wanted to stay with him and his wife so badly, but I didn't want to be a burden. I hated feeling like a hassle to anyone. And as much as I wanted a normal life, "normal" scared the hell out of me because I didn't know how to handle it. Instead of clinging to normal, it made me want to run fast in the other direction. My normal was always being scared, defensive and having anxiety about what was going to happen next.

In hindsight, I know that I clung to my anxiety stemming from my not-normal life because it was a security blanket for me. If I had normal, and gave up the security blanket, what would I have had left? The constant chaos around me distracted me from some of the most painful things of my life, and kept me occupied from thinking about Mom and so many of the other tragic things that had happened to me in my short life. Without the chaos, all of that would have hurt a lot more then what Larry and my sister was doing to me. And in all honesty, I didn't want to leave my sister. I did what she said not just because I was scared of her, but because I didn't want to lose her too. Normal just isn't something I have given myself in this life.

As I sat in that room waiting to listen to the woman tell me about her adoption experience, I had a few moments to think things over. I wished I had taken Mr. Boaz up on his generous offer, but it was too late now. I felt like a caged animal. My heart was racing, I could feel the tension throughout my body. A woman walked in the room then and my guard was up. I'm guessing she was in her late 20's; she was tall and slender, and she was dressed professionally in a pair of slacks and a dress shirt. She carried her big black brief case. I hated everything about her; she was the complete opposite of everything I was. I even hated the way her high heels sounded as they hit the tile floor as she walked towards me. It sounded like she was walking in slow motion.

I am pretty sure I purposely blocked out most of the words shared between us that day. Mostly what I remember sitting there thinking about what was the quickest way out of that room and away from that person. My motherly instincts were kicking in again: protect, defend, and escape were my goals, and the only thing I could think to do was to kick this lady where it hurt. Without going into the horrible details of our conversation, I will just tell you she left crying. This is the first time I realized I could make someone cry simply by using my words! It wasn't something I was proud of, but I was a mother trying to protect my child. Even that moment served a purpose. Eventually I realized that, as important as it was to know I could make someone cry and feel absolutely horrible with my words, I could do the complete opposite too. With my words, I can make someone happy, feel safe, and feel like they have purpose. With my words I can change a perspective or make someone's life better.

I know the lady came there that day to help me and try to convince me to do what she thought was best for me and my baby. She had no idea what I had already been through or who I was and this is a mistake many people make when trying to help others. Allowing your information to come through and presenting it to people is all you can do. Whenever helping someone else, no matter how old they are, you have to remember it is their life path and what they have chosen before they even came here. Our feelings are our guide to where we need to be and how we need to find our lessons in life.

When the information is presented to you and you feel compelled to act upon it, you will know it is time for a change. You know where you are supposed to be in life and when you have learned your lesson from the situation, it will be easy to move forward. When others are there telling you to get out of your situation, it is because they love you and don't want to see you hurt. They don't like how your situation makes them feel and the easiest thing for them to do is to tell you how to change. Even if they know first-hand what you are going through, they can be too eager for you to move on or do something, like give up your baby, when you know it just isn't right for you. Adoption is in some people's life plan, but it just wasn't in mine or my baby's.

Learn to analyze your own situation for what it is: a reflection of your own beliefs. Remember there is nothing outside of yourself. Even the people telling you what to do, are being created from your own mind. Take everything that is happening around you into consideration. After that moment of talking with that lady and making her cry, I knew this baby was mine and it took someone trying to convince me otherwise to appreciate that certainty. As long as I cared for my baby and loved her, no one would ever be able to take her from me.

There were a few more times when others would give me the opportunity to back out of being responsible for my child. The absolute worst was when Larry told me he knew someone who would sell her on the black market and "we" would get lots of money for her. I was horrified he would even suggest such a thing and didn't want to believe he was serious. After I freaked out about it he said he was joking, but somewhere deep down I think I knew he wasn't. To me it was something you don't even joke about anyway. Looking back now I have asked myself why I would create something so awful. The answer is, even Larry had a purpose. I learned a lot about myself from

Larry and being with him. Most importantly, because of him, I have my two oldest children.

The stress I was under during my pregnancy finally took its toll on me. The further along I progressed through pregnancy, the more insensitive Larry became. I had no idea what going into labor would feel like and I kept experiencing what I thought were contractions. It was just false labor, but Larry would get very angry at me when I would ask him to take me to the hospital. The first time it happened, he made me sit through his softball game before he would take me. I was in so much pain and felt so sick. At the hospital I learned I was having a gall bladder attack along with false contractions; I had over forty stones in my gall bladder! I believe all physical ailments are caused by emotional issues manifesting themselves into the solid world. According to the book *Your Body is Telling You: Love Yourself!* by Lise Bourbeau, stones are manifested from repression of anger and that repression can cause depression and bitterness. It goes on to say that you feel powerless and you don't get along with people who "fly off the handle" and you value self-control. This describes how I felt back then so perfectly.

After a long eight and a half months, I was starting to have complications with my pregnancy and my baby was in danger. The doctor decided to induce labor. I was terrified and confused, but I did it! On May 14th 1992, my oldest daughter was born and this healthy, 6 pound 7 ounce, beautiful little girl came into my life. I jumped right into being a mother as if I had been created for it. Haley was a perfect baby, she even slept through the night. I knew life at home wasn't going to be perfect for her though, and I couldn't stand to raise her around my sister. I also knew my sister had the ability to find another babysitter since she had found a sitter for the kids while I was at school. Of course she might have to pay for it, but she could do it.

I was so proud of my baby I wanted to show her off to anyone who would pay attention. I even thought of Vern, my ex stepdad, and how

I hadn't seen him for a couple of months. I didn't even tell him I was pregnant and during my last couple of months of pregnancy I avoid being around him. I got Haley ready and Larry was going to take us to his house. My brother's wife showed up unexpectedly right before we left. She told me Vern had passed away the day after Haley was born. I was dumb founded no one had bothered to even tell me he had been sick. I ignored my feelings about Vern dying and went on with my life.

In the first two weeks after Haley was born, I found myself at Larry's house more and more. Larry still lived with his mom and she wanted Haley and me to come stay with them. My sister wasn't happy I was gone, it meant she had to finally face her own responsibilities. She still went out and still worked a lot, and I still got to see the kids, but things were different now; the kids and I weren't trapped there anymore. As I settled into a new way of life, I was yet again deluded in thinking moving on meant moving into something better. But I was about to find out things could get a lot worse.

CHAPTER 3

ROCK BOTTOM

"Poisonous relationships can alter our perception. You can spend many years thinking you are worthless…but you're not worthless, you're unappreciated." [Steve Maraboli]

I moved in with Larry and immediately after leaving my sister's house, I knew I should not have. Literally overnight, my life went from worse to worst and, not for the first time, I began considering I had inherited Mom's poor judgment related to men. Larry, who had been mentally and emotionally abusive throughout our relationship, began physically abusing me as well once I moved in with him.

Yes, you read correctly: I do believe I *inherited* a propensity towards judging men accurately, but I am not referring necessarily to genetic inheritance. This is the kind of trait inherited by a child when they are raised observing abuse. Like carving a pattern into clay, the beliefs that abuse is how a woman should be treated by a man run deep below the surface and become a part of the clay. I believe these sorts of roots run much more deeply than simply being molded by our environment, as in the age-old discussion of nature vs. nurture, because the root of abuse (both perpetrating it and being accepting of it) can often be traced back through multiple generations within a family. The thread of abuse pervades each new generation, lifetime after lifetime.

The fact that abuse threads its way through subsequent generations is, I believe, proof of exactly how fragile the subconscious mind is. Way back then, when I was being abused by Larry, if someone had tried to explain to me why I thought and felt like being treated so horrible was right, maybe I would have been able to walk away a little easier. But I didn't have that voice of reason; all I had was a continuation of a thread from my mother's life that convinced my subconscious mind that abuse is okay. Once you expose the reason behind why you do certain things, it helps transform the habit. Old habits can be hard to break, but getting to the root of the issue is like killing the nerve of a root; this helps it become numb and able to be transformed.

If you are being abused, it is extremely possible that you were exposed to witnessing a woman you loved be abused by a man, either physically or mentally, at some point in your life. Of course, this isn't always the case, but from my observations it is true more often than not. Watching this behavior not only makes us more accepting of such behavior when it is inflicted on us, it actually also hardwires our brains to seek out that kind of attention. It's not even a matter of thinking it is okay, it is a matter of craving being treated in a demeaning manner.

The logical part of you says, "This is wrong and I know I deserve to be treated decently!" Unfortunately, 'logical' goes right out the window when it is in conflict with your belief system. So, in order to feel loved you think you need to receive negative attention. Your subconscious mind might pick a man who treats you badly because, you rationalize, if he takes the time out of his day to treat you badly, this is proof to you that he knows you exist. Also, you rationalize, a man who treats you with respect must not love you as he just isn't that concerned enough with you to take the time to treat you badly. He doesn't care about you if he isn't concerned with controlling your life or physically isn't putting effort into paying attention to you by hurting you.

Lest I miss the opportunity to say this very clearly, please know this: there are *never any good excuses* for letting someone treat you this way. Abuse in all forms and fashions, in any circumstances, is *always* wrong. That said, I understand from experience what tricks our subconscious mind plays on us, and all the so-called 'good

FINDING THE ROAD TO REASON

reasons' for accepting abuse in a relationship. This is the reason I am able to say, look at your history, your family history and relationship history, as a way of beginning to help yourself recognize patterns of accepting abuse. This is an important way to help yourself add back an element of logic in a not-so-logical situation when your brain and your subconscious mind are at odds.

Looking back at my own story, I will continue by saying that I knew it was wrong to let Larry abuse me, but for all the reasons we just discussed, I could not admit this to myself logically. Also, my reasons for accepting his abuse took another turn. That is, the more he abused me, the more I felt justified in feeling sorry for myself. It wasn't that his abuse made me feel better, but it made something inside me feel right. The more he wronged me, the more sympathy I could get from others. It felt good to have someone feel sorry for me. I thought my role as a woman was to be pushed around and test out the limits of how much pain I could endure, physically and mentally.

By living with Larry and his mom, he exerted more control over me than he ever had before. He knew I couldn't and didn't want to go back to Cindy's and that I couldn't get a place of my own. So, just like Mom, I was stuck with someone I did not love. During the time I spent with Larry, I didn't have goals or healthy pursuits. Rather, the effort I could have spent in pursuing normal and healthy goals in my youth was wasted on thinking of ways to survive.

Of course, I could not have admitted that to myself at the time as much of what I have learned is only visible to me in my own rearview mirror. In fact, at the time, I would probably have told you that I was living a very normal life. I went back to school, for example, when Haley was about five months old. Very normal, right?

There was nothing normal about it, though. I had horrible anxiety about leaving her during the day. My thoughts were obsessive when I was away from her and I worried constantly that something devastating was happening to her. I think most of it was with good reason since it was Larry who was watching her for even just a short time each day until his mom got home from working in the morning.

My return to school did not last long. I dropped out when Larry's mom told me she came home and Larry was sleeping while Haley was wide away in her walker and she had pulled everything off the table. My thoughts became frantic thinking of all the things that could have happened. She could have rolled her way into some real danger. I was grateful all she did was mess up some papers, but I wasn't going to take a chance on something horrible happening to her. I chose instead to officially become a stay-at-home mom. Larry liked it that way because he didn't have to worry about me having as much contact with my friends and other people.

When I was seventeen, Larry and I found a small house to buy about half a block away from his mom. Everything had to be in his name, he insisted, even our car. Not having anything in my name was just another way he could control everything and control become a crucial element of his abuse towards me.

Now that we weren't in his mom's house, he began to hit me more and more. I never knew if something I said or did was going to set him off or "push his buttons," as he would say. Mendy and Mary would still come to see me once in a while, but Larry looked for every opportunity to tear my friendships apart. He told them lies about me; he convinced Mary I had turned her in for neglecting her children; and even my lifelong friend Mendy turned on me because of vicious lies that were spread, though at the time I had no idea Larry was undermining me this way.

With no one left in the world besides Larry, my sister and Larry's mom, I felt the walls closing in on me. He would get very obsessed about me leaving the house and about where I was going. I couldn't even talk on the phone without him accusing me of talking bad about him. Even if someone called and hung up or if it was a wrong number, he would yell at me and claim he knew it was another man calling me. He didn't ever want to work and would only keep a job for a couple of weeks at a time, giving some excuse as to why he quit or got fired. Mostly he would claim everyone at work, no matter where he worked, was out to get him. His Mom paid most of our bills for us and bought Haley diapers and anything she needed. I was grateful for his mom's help, but it just enabled Larry and I to stay stuck in our abnormal cycle, the cycle we came to know as our normal life.

Though my motivation to keep going in life was still my child, over time I began feeling as though there was so much more out there waiting for me. There was more to my life than what I was doing with it. I recall beginning to feel as though there was always something missing, though I could not put my finger on exactly what it was. I was certain though that the life I was living was not the normal life I had imagined for Haley and I also began to recognize that staying with Larry just to be certain she had a dad in her life was not getting her any closer to the normal I wanted for her.

Larry didn't want much to do with Haley unless there were others around to see he was giving her attention. He wouldn't change diapers or any of the other numerous responsibilities that are required of parents of small children. I didn't mind taking on all the tasks, the chores, the responsibility; I enjoyed being Haley's Mom. I admit I had the attitude if I didn't do it, it would not have been done right, but Larry didn't want to be a dad anyway so I don't believe this attitude was harmful to our defunct relationship.

As time went on, Larry's and my relationship continued to get worse. I hated him more and more with each passing day and over time, we no longer even slept in the same bedroom. Haley and I slept in one room and he slept in the other. My depression continued with no sign of letting up and I know it wasn't because of Larry and the way he treated me. On the contrary, everything I was going through with him was just a manifestation, or what I call a side effect, of the beliefs I held at the time, which caused great sadness. The more I wished I could get out, the more I was creating what I didn't want. It was like being trapped in a locked cage, or quick sand. The more I struggled, the more trapped I became. At the time I believed it was Larry who held the key to my cage; now I know that I held the key all along. Actually, I didn't even need a key at all to escape my prison; all I had to do was look up to see the top was wide open, if I could only believe it was so.

As Larry's abuse became more intense, I became more and more shut-in. By that I mean that Larry's obsessive ideas about me became paranoid delusions. He started doing things like marking the tires on the car so he would know if I went anywhere. He would threaten me by saying that since the car was in his name, if I left the house in it or even thought about leaving, he would call the cops and say I stole it. If I talked about driving, he would hit me. Just like Pavlov's dog would automatically salivate when hearing the bell, soon even thoughts about driving made me anxious and getting behind the steering wheel would make me throw up. I couldn't go anywhere unless Larry or Larry's mom took me; if I did, I would pay dearly.

Not only was I sad, I felt so pathetic and worthless during this time in my life. I wanted so badly to escape the world, but the habit of being terrified froze me in our tiny little house in Evansdale, Iowa. Again I found myself stuck, day after day I ran into myself and ran into Larry. When I was honest with myself, I could admit that every day I felt like I had an itch I couldn't locate and satisfy. I would sit on the step of the house and look at the car sitting there, knowing it was freedom. I would ask myself how someone could have so much control over one person. How could someone allow someone else this much control? I daydreamed about where I would go and the things Haley and I would do if I could just get in the car and drive away.

I recognized that from the time Mom passed away, someone else had always been in control of my life. First it was my sister Deb, then

Cindy, then Larry. Because of this it is possible that without my even knowing it, somewhere deep inside my mind I had decided I wasn't any good at being in charge of my world. I had already let my own mother die and it seemed like every choice I had made so far turned out the complete opposite of what was good and right and normal and healthy.

Cindy still had her hands in the pot too. She definitely needed me way more then I needed her. She loved that I was with Larry because she knew where I was going to be all the time. She knew I would not have any plans. I watched her kids daily, even on the weekends. To her it didn't matter how much I had the kids because I had nothing else to do. She got over being mad about me leaving, only because she realized now she could drop her kids off and go. When she needed to, she would always find a way to justify being away from her kids. I wanted to be my niece and nephew's aunt, not their everyday care giver. The frustration of being so young and having so many adult responsibilities weighed heavy on my mind and over time, the need to control my environment became overwhelming.

I had no idea at the time, but feeling so out of control of what was happening to me manifested itself into becoming a compulsive cleaner. There were times I would stay up all night until morning scrubbing the kitchen floor. The rest of the house could be a normal mess, maybe even small hoards here and there, but I would spend hours down on the floor with whatever scrubbing device I could find detailing the floor until it was spotless.

I often write about reality being a reflection of the subconscious mind and this is especially true about your immediate environment. A revealing way to tell what kind of state the subconscious mind is in is to look at the spaces around you. That kitchen floor represented the tiny part of my mind I was in control of. Somewhere there was a piece of my mind that was sane and clean and made sense. The rest of my mind was an unorganized mess and no matter how much I tried to keep it cleaned up, I could not find a way to keep everything from falling and being a mess.

I call myself a closet hoarder. By that I mean, my house might be clean but, at least back in those days, if you opened my closets you would find them packed full of useless items. The closets were a physical manifestation of the invisible closets of my mind, packed full of issues I didn't want to deal with. I have gotten into the habit now of cleaning out my closets and cupboards every now and again, but they always seem to get filled back up. When I transform my limited beliefs and work on my issues, my physical environment becomes easier to organize. The state of your house, car, garage, where you work or even your closets, are the easiest way to know when you need transformation. Just like my closets contain my mess sometimes, everything around you is a representation of certain parts of your mind.

When I am thinking back and writing about what happened, it is easy to see how my environment was a manifestation of my mind. At the time and when you are living in it, it is hard to see what you are creating around you and why. I encourage everyone to write down what has happened to them. Not to relive it over and over or so it can be read again and again, but to allow it to become solid somewhere so your mind can begin to let go of it. If your mind knows your traumatic experiences are located somewhere in a solid way, it can stop reflecting on them and worrying about trying to manifest them in your physical world.

There is a reason people have been searching for and finding ways to express themselves in a number of ways, such as through writing or symbols, since the beginning of mankind's history. It is because what is inside the mind will always find a way to manifest itself in the "real" world.

For me paper and pen became as dear as old friends, the kind who were always waiting for me to share and give them life. When no one else cared about what happened to me, my notebook was always there to make me feel better. I am not quite sure what I would have done if I never had the ability or opportunity to express myself through words. The notebook was there even when I failed at life. I definitely failed at having the guts to get out. Every once in a great while, I would work up the nerve to try to ask for help. I would talk to Larry's mom about being abused, but she would just tell me, "If you leave, it will give Larry's grandpa a heart attack!"

I had grown very fond of Larry's grandpa, Harold, and I am sure he liked having me around too. He and I become family. He would come over sometimes and keep me company by telling me stories from when he was younger, or he would fall asleep on my couch watching T.V. I loved talking to him and he taught me how to fix things around the house. I also knew when he was around Larry and I wouldn't be fighting and I wouldn't have to worry about getting hit. I didn't want to hurt Harold or make him worry about Haley and I. Somewhere in my mind I knew I probably wouldn't give him a heart attack by leaving, but I was scared to death to be on my own.

The feeling of not wanting to be alone to take care of everything by myself terrified me enough that I accepted the abuse and isolation. As long as Haley and I had each other we would be fine. My belief was, life was meant for surviving until something happened to make you have to fight to live. I was noble for staying and the more I had to put up with, the more the world could see me as being strong. Strength is what I prayed for every night. Prayer can be important if done properly, but I had it all wrong. I kept praying for strength and just kept getting more and more situations that required me to be strong. The more I prayed and cried to God the worse the abuse became.

It didn't take long for my life to become even more of a pity party. When I was nineteen I became pregnant with my second child. I hoped my prayers had been answered and the abuse would stop, since I was pregnant.

I was wrong again and the abuse just got worse. I think an unwanted dog would have been treated better than I was. Again I was horribly sick during my pregnancy, making my depression worse. I began to lose a lot of weight and could barely get out of bed in the morning. It took all my energy just to get up and take care of Haley and watch my niece and nephew. Doing normal or everyday things like shoveling snow from the driveway or doing dishes made me feel like I just wanted to die. Some days were better than others, but not too many. Larry was not happy at all about the way I felt. He called me lazy even though I still did all my chores. He made me feel like I was just being a baby and I would think to myself, "What is wrong with you? Women have babies all the time and still do all kinds of things!" He would say derogatory things like, "Good job holding down the couch so it don't fly away." I guess it was his job to sleep all day and stay up all night playing on the computer or playing video games.

I realized when I was about seven months pregnant and he broke a kitchen chair over my back that I was probably going to end up dead in that house. There was nothing sacred to Larry, not even being pregnant, and he didn't love or care about me. It was almost like he was doing everything he could to get me to leave him.

The belief that if a man treats you like crap he loves you, had slowly but surely fallen apart in my mind. I began to despise Larry and his ideas about how to treat me. I no longer wanted his attention. Having purpose in being a mother meant I was important to someone. That was just enough of the confidence I needed to realize I deserved so much better. I was still just surviving, but the thought of there being more to life for my children and myself kept growing stronger. I started to feel the cords of attachment between Larry and I dissolve and my focus became more about escaping than trying to learn to live with the abuse.

I set an immediate goal, a short-term goal, but an important one: get through my pregnancy with my baby alive. I did whatever I needed to accommodate Larry and not push his buttons anymore. Even when Larry informed me he wasn't ready to be a dad again, I held my tongue. In my mind I was thinking, "You dumbass; it is kind of late to be worried about becoming a dad when you have one child and a baby on the way!" A statement like that would have gotten me into trouble, so for my baby's safety I kept my mouth shut.

Something about this pregnancy changed me and it was more than just the physical changes. Through it, I developed a different attitude and as I changed and started to let go of my door mat tendencies, things around me began to change. My sister Cindy announced that her husband had gotten transferred to North Carolina and they would be moving. My first thought was about the kids and how badly I would miss them. Then I realized I wouldn't be babysitting anymore and thought I this might make my life a little easier, but instead something about it made me sad. Once my sister moved, it felt lonely without the kids, but I still had Haley and my pregnancy to keep me occupied. When she moved my sister and I actually started to have more of a real relationship. We would write letters back and forth and she had become pregnant with her third child. Her husband had a good job and was making more money. Cindy would even send me a little money now and then, something she had never done for me even when I lived with her. I thought for sure she was growing up and becoming the person I knew she really was. Although she had moved so far away I had my big sister back. She was strong and did not let alcohol control her anymore.

To this day I still have those letters to remind me of the sister I once had. It only lasted a couple of months, then they were back. Like Mom had said long before, "You can leave, but you always end up back here." While they looked for a new place to live, my sister and her family stayed at our house. Living in the same house again with my sister, and both of us pregnant, was not a good idea. Our tiny little house became even smaller as the tension grew thicker by the day. Luckily before a nuclear explosion happened they found a place. I didn't have the kind loving sister anymore; she had been left back in North Carolina. I wondered if the changes I was seeing in my own attitudes would be equally fleeting changes, or if by some miracle the strength I was gaining could be a permanent change in my life.

CHAPTER 4

STARTING TO FIND MY STRENGTH

"We all learn lessons in life. Some stick, some don't. I have always learned more from rejection and failure than from acceptance and success." [Henry Rollins]

Cindy and her family moved out shortly before my due date, at the end of May. My due date came and went and I was the typical miserable pregnant woman. Each day that passed was more miserable then the next, and every day began with me fervently hoping today was the day my baby would decide to come, and every day ended with disappointment. I was sure my baby was never going to want to get out! Thinking about it now I realize if I was that tiny little baby, hearing what was going on in the outside world, I probably would have never wanted to leave either.

This is an excerpt from my journal at that time, a time when I was so naïve: *"I have just turned 19 yrs. old. I am about to have my second child. 19 yrs. ago I was safe with my mother in her arms. I wonder if I had known what the world was going to be like if I would have decided to be born. Did I want to hide away from the world and never want to come out or was I excited to face the challenges ahead? Does my baby know what kind of place it will be born into?"*

On Growth and Change

It doesn't matter how long we try to hide from the world, as long as we continue to grow, either physically or through enlightenment, life will happen. Just like my baby tried to fight growth, we can fight it too. However, because growth is change and change is a force which can never be stopped, it will happen in spite of us. The only thing left for you to decide, then, is, are you in control of the changes or are they happening on default?

If you allow change, embrace it and are aware of it, it will work for you. If you object to it and try to force it to stop, what will manifest are all your doubts and fears about life. They manifest because in the back of your mind you are running scenarios of "what if?" on automatic. Even if you don't know it, those thoughts are running over and over. Those thoughts running in the back of your mind put you in a constant "flight" mode, a mode in which your entire body and mind is in a never-ending state of panic even when there is no real threat. Could my own state of panic been keeping me from having my baby? Maybe it could have been my tiny little baby was already refusing to live in a world that was so chaotic. To this day, she is very outspoken and stubborn; it is part of who she is.

For whatever reason, I continued to stay pregnant and these were days that taught me patience. I also learned everything happens in its own time. The day my daughter decided to be born was part of her story and it needed to occur exactly the way it did in order to be the right beginning for her. She and I share the story of her birth, it is unique to us as the story of birth between a mother and a child always is. It is this shared story that creates such a strong sense of belonging between a mother and her baby because no two people will ever share the same story exactly in the same way.

My daughter might not realize how special her birth is to me. It is important not just because she is as special as any of my other children, but because this was a time in my life when I realized I was something more than how others treated me. This was a big lesson for me and I learned it because of her. I also learned I did care what people thought of me and how I wanted them to see me in this world.

Becoming a Mother Again

The date my second child was forced out of her own comfort zone, the day Mother Nature prevailed over her stubbornness, was June 18th 1995, Father's Day.

I had been having many false contractions all through the night and into the morning. It wasn't much of a concern to me because I had dealt with that throughout my pregnancy. Larry continued to sleep while I suffered through each and every single one. I remember it was extremely hot and Larry's mom had just bought us a window air conditioner. I had positioned myself right in front of the air to help ease some of my discomfort. Then things worsened, I felt worse and worse, and some additional symptoms presented. Growing concerned, I called the hospital and spoke to a nurse there who recommended I come in. My thoughts weren't just centered on the pain I was in, I was also worried about Larry getting up to take me to the hospital and being in false labor. I didn't want him to get mad and do something to punish me for the inconvenience and have him hurt my baby. I debated on waking him up for just a moment, and then I worked up the guts to do it. I said, "Please get up and take me to the hospital." He mumbled, "You're not in labor; we will go later."

I took a deep breath and decided I wasn't going to push it; I would wait. Only I couldn't wait much longer. The pain became increasing worse. I was so angry that Larry wouldn't wake up, and frustrated that Larry's mom, who had taken Haley the night before, wasn't answering the phone. In that moment, my fear of leaving without him or his mom melted away. I didn't care anymore and the anxiety of it just fell away.

Not being worried about what Larry was going to do to me was the first taste of real freedom I had in a long time, but I was too busy to enjoy it. I started to panic, knowing I needed to get to the hospital. I couldn't think for a moment and then I remembered I have a sister and a brother. I didn't know if I would be able to get ahold of them, but

I had to try. My last resort would be finding the car keys and driving myself, but that idea made me panic even more. I grabbed the phone and I called my sister, praying that she would pick up the phone. Luckily she picked up right away and I was relieved when she said she was on her way to get me.

During my wait for a ride I hoped Larry would not wake up for anything and I could just go to the hospital and have my baby without him knowing. I didn't want him there to be a part of it. He wasn't going to share in my happiness to meet our child, so why would I want him there? Larry never woke up and I was able to sneak out unnoticed.

Cindy pulled up in the drive way and our brother was in the car with her. Upon seeing them, a great deal of weight was lifted off my shoulders. On the way to the hospital we laughed and joked around like real siblings do. I knew they were keeping my mind off things and maybe they even felt a little sorry for me because Larry was such a jerk. I was happy to be on my way, even though part of me was in doubt and thought I was going to get sent home. What if I did get sent home? Would Larry understand for once, or would he freak out? I remember thinking if I was just having false labor, I could save the papers from the hospital to prove where I went and what time I was there. Now safe, I could feel myself starting to go back into fear mode.

There is a shame that comes along with letting someone treat you the way Larry treated me, but I had a taste of what it was like to be me again. That bold, confident, know-it-all girl I had left a long time ago had come back, for just a second. She was the one who cared about me and knew I was worth being treated right.

Once in the hospital and after my examination, I realized exactly how close I was to having my baby at home. I called Larry's mom and explained to her I was in the hospital and in labor. She asked how Larry was and I told her he was at home sleeping. That was a big mistake because she went over and woke him up. Not long after I hung up with

Larry's mom, I was being prepared to have my baby. I looked over at the door; someone walking through it had caught my eye. It was Larry and by the look on his face, he was pissed. He glared at me as he walked across the room to a reclining chair on the other side of my bed. He plopped down in the chair, kicked it out and closed his eyes as if he was going to continue his slumber. The nurse looked at me and asked if he was the father. Putting my head down so I wouldn't have to look directly at her and as quite as I possibly could I said, "Yes."

In a very loud and stern voice the nurse said to Larry, "You need to get up, she is ready to have this baby!" I just wanted him to stay sleeping so I wouldn't have to feel the anger coming off of his soul. Unfortunately, with a huge sigh, he got up and stood next to my bed. Just a few moments later, Alexandria was born. Larry took a look at her and walked out. I was slightly dazed from just having given birth and was not quite aware of where he went or even if he came back; I was just happy my baby was fine and healthy.

After an extremely hard night of trying to calm an excessively fussy baby and many failed attempts at breast feeding, I was ready to go home. I only had to stay for a short time; I think it was barely 24 hours. The doctor came up right away to check on us and give my daughter a special gift. He handed me a savings bond for her and gave me half a smile. He told me I did a good job. I think his words were more special to me than the gift he had given my baby. No one had told me I did a "good job" in labor and something about hearing these simple words of compassion and congratulations melted me.

Now that I was being released to go home, I called Larry. "Come get us, we can go home," I said. He replied with, "In a little bit," and hung up the phone. I knew he wasn't making a rush to get there, so I decided I would take Alex down to the nursery and take a bath before I left.

As we walked slowly down the hall there were many other rooms with women and babies in them. Each room seemed to be decorated with flowers, balloons, and cards. There was even one room which had a huge stuffed dog sitting there looking like he had purpose. I envied all them for just a moment until I looked down and realized what I had. I had the cutest baby in the whole place. She had thick, long, dark brown hair. Her hair was so long nurses from all around the ward kept coming in to see her. She looked at me with her beautiful huge eyes and she had a tiny button nose. She was perfect and she was all mine. I wasn't jealous of any of them anymore. I felt the smile on my face as I continued to walk, knowing I would get compliments about how cute she was way longer then their gifts would last. I might not have been special enough for presents, but God gave me the most special gift ever, my Alex.

Larry didn't pick us up until that evening. I was mad he would leave us there that long and I told him all about it. His mom tried to make me feel bad about my anger, saying she couldn't pick us up because she was cleaning our house. It made me even madder because I didn't need my house cleaned; I had spent months nesting and preparing the house for my baby. She decided while I was in the hospital that it was time to have all my curtains cleaned. They didn't even finish the job. Some of my curtains lay on the kitchen table wet.

Shortly after we arrived home, Larry's mom left and there we stood, Haley, Larry, and me. Alex lay in her car seat crying her head off. I made another attempt at breast feeding and by this time it was growing more painful by the second. As I was struggling in my attempt at feeding Alex, Larry told me, "I am leaving. I am going out with some friends." My jaw dropped in disbelief. Was he really leaving me there to take care of the kids by myself, forty-eight hours after giving birth? I had just had a baby, was sore from head to toe, and he was going to go party with some new friends he had made God only knows where. He didn't even bother to hold his baby once before he left. He just walked out the door. I knew he wouldn't have helped me much anyway, so in a way I was happy he was gone.

I stayed up all night with Alex as she screamed and cried. It seemed like she was hungry, but she wouldn't eat. Around four in the morning, Larry came in. Out of frustration and exhaustion I yelled, "Where have you been all night? I could have used your help!" Luckily Haley had been able to sleep through Alex's big baby fit, but I still could have used some support from somewhere. Larry gave me a mean nasty look and said, "I went fishing."

"Yeah, sure you did!" I replied. "With no poles or any fishing stuff?"

He continued to give me the evil eye, then laid down on the couch with his back towards me and sarcastically said, "Good night." I'm still not sure what made me so shocked about his actions, but at the time I was very shocked. I lashed out at him. "You're not going to help me with the baby?" I said. He just laid there, silent, acting like he couldn't hear me or Alex. I sat and looked at him lying on the couch with the echoing sound of my baby crying. I began to realize exactly how mean this person was.

I realized in that moment that I deserved so much better, my children deserved so much better and I knew I was now on a mission to make our lives what they should be. I promised Alex that night that I would do what I could to make her life better.

As soon as eight o'clock rolled around the following morning and the doctor's office opened, I called right away to ask the doctor for advice. I think he could tell I was very sad and frustrated and he already knew I was all alone. He told me, "Go get her a bottle and some formula and give her that." I felt like I failed my baby by not being able to hang in there and keep breast feeding, but now I know under the circumstances it was probably what was best. Although I was disappointed in myself, I was relieved when the doctor told me to feed her with the bottle. I went to Larry and said without hesitation, "Larry, get up! I need a ride to the store to get Alex a bottle and formula!" He just laid there as if he didn't hear me. I continued to bug him about it until he answered me.

"No, I will do it when I get up!" he yelled.

I knew that could mean later that night or if he was sleeping really well, the next day. Alex was still crying at this point so he put the pillow over his head and continued to sleep. Larry's mom was at work and would not be home for at least an hour or two, so we had to wait. As soon as she came home she picked the kids and I up. Alex cried her way to the store, through the store and all the way home. As soon as I got that bottle, she finally ate her fill and she slept for a couple of hours. Of course I couldn't sleep because Haley was up, but the silence was enough relief for me.

What I Learned

Those first few days with Alex taught me how to be resilient and what I *didn't want* in a partner. More importantly, I learned how to love myself a little more. I hated that period of time and, to this day, just thinking about it makes me so angry. Then I remember why I had to go through a moment like that: in my near future there was something greater coming that would build on what I had learned in those moments, and those firsthand and difficult experiences in Alex's first days created something in me that started shaping me into who I needed to be.

I also look back and recognize that, in my contract, I didn't give myself all these trials just so I could sit around feeling sorry for myself someday. I did it to make me stronger. Everything happening leading up to each time I learned something, happened for a reason. Each little reason contributed to the big reason, to a bigger lesson. It doesn't mean I have accepted what I allowed Larry to do to me, but it does mean I take responsibility for it. Not all the time just when I feel like it and when I want things in my life to go a little smoother. I admit fully that I don't always remember I am not a victim.

After the birth of our daughter I realized exactly what Larry was. He was self-centered and was not who I wanted to spend the rest of my life with. His mistreatment of me was just going to continue to get worse. Why wouldn't it? I was allowing him to treat me that way, regardless of whether or not I allowed it out of fear. It doesn't matter why I allowed it, the fact is I *did* allow it. The longer I stayed, the more my thoughts became obsessed with thinking of ways to leave him or get him to leave us.

I now know the more I could challenge my beliefs about how a man should treat a woman, the faster Larry would not be an issue in my life. My beliefs were what kept me there and controlled me, not him. He was solid evidence of what I thought a man was and I didn't want those beliefs anymore. The more I resisted and spoke up, the harder my beliefs would fight to keep me believing what was true in my world. The subconscious mind doesn't do this to hurt us. It would be like asking a computer to care when, where, or how you gave it purpose. The subconscious mind is like a computer with a program to protect you. It doesn't have any feelings as to how to protect you, it just knows the programing. We set most of the programs ourselves long before we even know what is good and bad in this world.

There were so many beliefs in that specific program I was running at the time; and the more beliefs you have, the stronger it becomes. It may seem strange that the subconscious mind thought getting abused would protect me. That program secured me a mate in this world, my programing meant I was loved, and it meant there was someone there and I wouldn't be alone. As I said earlier in this book, "alone" is a big one for me personally, and is a root belief.

There are other programs for survival too, though, and yours may be different. There is one that says, "If I get hit hard enough, I could die." Getting hurt daily and being in pain was chaotic and depressing, which was caused by the conflict in different programs. When our programs or beliefs become so physical, sometimes the only way to deal with it is actually in the physical. For me that meant actually physically leaving, but I had to work up the nerve first.

As much as I thought about wanting him to leave me, I knew he never would. It was like it was his mission to make me feel horrible. I secretly saved up every single bit of change I could find in hopes someday I might have enough money to get out. When I think about it now, I kind of chuckle at the idea that money was the reason why I couldn't get out. Even if I did have the money and a car, it would not have mattered because I was terrified to drive, terrified to be alone and didn't see any logical way out of my situation.

Larry continued his abuse towards me and I continued to push his buttons. I also continued to pray and pray, wondering when God would answer. He was answering. Just like Mom had said, "God always answers". God was silently watching and waiting for me to find my strength. If God had a voice, He would have said, "Hang on, you are going to get this." Maybe He would have told me He was going to need me to write a series of books someday, because someone out there would read it and know it was a message from Him.

CHAPTER 5

AFTER THE STORM

"The little reed, bending to the force of the wind, soon stood upright again when the storm had passed over." [Aesop]

I ended the previous chapter by sharing that I know God intended for me to help others through my experiences. And I know that this is the reason He allowed me to go through so many of the things I did, for long periods of time when I was praying to Him to remove me from my circumstances. This was all for the purpose of someday being able to write these things to you and serve as a messenger for good, a messenger to tell you about the Universal Laws. Do I say this in order to convince you I am something special, a prophet or teacher of sorts? Absolutely not. Actually, I believe serving a purpose and contributing to the experience of the collective, greater good is *what we are all here for*.

You've heard it said before: what comes around goes around. To me this has come to mean that by helping someone, that help is going to come back around to me; how I make a person feel will be downloaded into the whole; and when I need to access the benefit of their experience, I can do that.

Sometimes the way we access it is through real life physical experience, and sometimes it can be as simple as having a good thought. Maybe some call that *karma*, or maybe another name; it doesn't matter what name you put to it, the energy is there for you to use. My belief is that someone out there will read my books and it will help them. The feeling someone gets when they have that "ah ha!" moment or when they realize they are not alone because of what I wrote is the good energy I am trying to create. I don't want to go around making people feel like Larry made me feel, because someday I might have to feel that too. I don't have all the answer to how this life thing works and my mind is always changing, but I do know I like making people feel good and when I make someone feel bad, that makes me feel bad because I am part of the whole, just like you.

I have been asked on more than one occasion where I pick up my ideas about life. Some of my thoughts just come to me, but more often than not they come through observation of things around me. Life imitates nature and this is where I get most of my information about how the universe works. For example, in nature if there is a bad storm and things are damaged, you can repair the damage, but it takes time and things are never the same again; the landscape is forever changed. Nature also knows that if something happens to one thing, good or bad, it will affect the whole forest in one way or another. The effects actually go beyond the forest and become less and less impactful the further the distance from the event, until it seems like nothing has happened at all.

My time with Larry was just like being right smack in the middle of a huge storm that just kept growing and growing. I continued begging God for help and although there were little things to keep me hoping, like being forced to get my G.E.D because we were on public assistance, it seemed like help was never coming. Finally, when I was twenty-one, hope flooded my life when I found out my father was still alive! I have written about my experience finding my father in my first book of this series, *Preacher's Li'l Secret.* That hope was short-lived though as, soon after, my father rejected me. Hope turned into disappointment and deepened my depression even further. I learned in the search for my father, as I shared in the first book of this series, that I did not have the kind of father who was going to rescue me from the mess my life had become, as I had always hoped my father would. If I was going to get out of this mess, I was going to have to do it another way.

Larry used my failure with my dad against me. He would often mention how my own father didn't even want anything to do with me and, sadly, there were times I believed in what he was saying. I felt like garbage and like maybe I did deserve to be treated horribly if my own father didn't want me. I came from him and he didn't want anything to do with me, so how could I expect others to want me around? For a moment I accepted that I was only worth something to people if I could do things for them. If I continued to be a good babysitter for my sister and punching bag for Larry, I had purpose. It just wasn't good enough for me to be me; I had to provide something or no one would want me in their world. The only ones I belonged to were my children and I worried that they also might not continue to love me as they grew older. What if, when they no longer needed me to serve and help them, they also found little value in me?

Thoughts bombarded my mind daily to the point they became so loud I could not sleep most nights. My mind would go through every possible solution towards fixing how bad I felt. The stress started to manifest itself physically and before I knew it, I was sick. I had back pain, my stomach issues became worse and the migraines never seemed to go away. At the time I still believed that my body and my mind, emotions, and beliefs were all separate. I felt like I was dying! I thought for sure there was something really wrong with my health. Physically I couldn't take it anymore and I made an appointment to see the doctor. Larry's mom took me the appointment that would change the rest of my life. I went in thinking I was going to be getting a dreary diagnosis; what I got instead was a shock!

My appointment began with the doctor asking me what was wrong. I began to tell her all my physical problems. As I explained in detail each problem I had, I could feel the tension draining from that part of my body. Before I knew it, I was in tears. The doctor, knowing there was much more to the tears than just the physical pain, asked me what was really wrong. It was those words from her that switched something on in my mind. All of a sudden I was telling her what hell I had been going through, how trapped I was and how much I couldn't see a way out of it. I shared with her every single detail of my awful life. She looked at me and told me, "I will be right back." I panicked and my heart started racing. What had I done?

A few minutes later, the doctor returned. I started to open my mouth to tell her I was just going to go home, but she spoke before I had the chance. "I can help you," she said, with confidence.

The panic went away and my ears perked up; I was ready to listen. The doctor handed me a card with a name and an appointment time written on it. As I looked down at the card in my hand, I heard her say, "This lady can help you and I am here for you too. She works here in our office." I got ready to open my mouth to tell her it wasn't possible for me to see a counselor because if Larry found out I would probably end up dead, but she stopped me from speaking. As if she knew what I was going to say, she explained to me she that would help me with Larry. If Larry questioned where I was she would provide me with proof that I was there in the office being treated for legitimate medical issues. She said, "He never has to know you are even seeing a counselor." With a half-smile I looked to her and said, "Okay. I will do it."

I tried to wipe the smile off my face before I got to the car where Larry's mom waited for me. She asked me how my appointment went and I said, "I have to go back." She just said, "Okay, let me know when and I will take you."

All the way home, my mind wandered. Already I was feeling different in some crucial way. Somehow I knew this was it, this was my way out. Like that first breath you take after swimming to the bottom of the pool and the relief you get when you get oxygen again, I felt the same way in that moment. My ailments had gone away for the time being, at least until I got home. I was nervous about lying to Larry about going to the counselor, but I knew if I could just get to that first appointment it would get easier.

Once I was back home Larry didn't ask me much about how my appointment went, and I didn't offer up any information. Now instead of thoughts about how I could get away, I was thinking about what my appointment with the counselor would be like. Would she really help me or would she just judge me? How could I make her understand how I felt? What I felt was embarrassing to discuss with someone, and I felt shame at having allowed someone to treat me the way Larry had. And, I was ashamed that I couldn't drive anymore. Everyone drives! It was like I was a little helpless baby and because I couldn't get out of the situation myself, I was also a failure.

I had a whole week to think of all kinds of things and to even talk myself out of going. As many excuses as there were to not go, there was one really important reason I went: for my kids. If I was going to do it for anyone, it was them and only them. They were the only reason I could find that was worth risking Larry finding out and worth overcoming the fear I had. I didn't want my girls to think this is what women are supposed to do with their lives. I didn't want them to think it was okay to be abused. I had to do it for them. I did it so they wouldn't have to watch their own mother be constantly sad. They deserved more, and so did I.

The day of the appointment came. I was nervous as I left the house that day. I was getting away with this once, but what would happen the next time if I had to go back? I checked in and then sat down in the waiting area. The door was right there, all I had to do was get up and walk back to the car where Larry's mom waited for me. Before I could even finish the thought of leaving, a tall, older woman in a floor length, colorful skirt and long sleeved top, with short, salt-and-pepper hair called my name. She smiled at me and I smiled back. I stood and walked towards the door and she introduced herself. "My name is

Ann," she said. We continued down the hall to her office.

My mind suddenly went blank. I was fearful she would ask what I needed help with, and the anxiety I felt in anticipating that question was palpable. I sat in a chair across from her and before I knew it, I was talking a mile a minute. The beginning of the conversation consisted of me talking about not being able to drive. When she asked me what my goals were for therapy, my answer was, "I want to be able to drive again." From there almost everything I had gone through in my life was exposed – my mom dying, the way my sisters had treated me, being abused by Larry, it all came out. It seemed to only have taken a few minutes to explain everything. It had been bottled up for so long it was like shaking a pop can and opening it up – there was an explosion of emotion and lots of tears. The image of me driving was a symbol of all the freedoms that I had lost and was taking back. When I said to Ann, "I want to be able to drive again," that one statement summed up all the devastation of my life, and flooded my soul.

Without hesitation the counselor started talking right when she needed to. Ninety percent of me expected her to just talk and the other ten percent hoped she had a magic pill in one of her desk drawers. I would not have cared if that pill was as big as a watermelon, I would have found a way to swallow it; I was desperate. As she talked, I watched as she moved around setting up a tripod in front of me. It had a metal bar attached to the top of it. The bar was about a foot and a half long and maybe a couple inches wide, with little tiny light bulbs on it. I didn't understand what she was doing at first. I must have had a curious look on my face because she began to explain to me what EMDR was.

You may have read about EMDR in my first book in this series. For those who haven't, I will briefly explain what it is here. Eye Movement Desensitization and Reprocessing (EMDR) helps to reprogram your brain after you have had traumatic events in your life. It makes the anxiety and fear disappear. For me it was the magic pill hidden in the desk drawer. I will leave it at that and explain my experience with it and how it helped me with my anxiety of driving.

At first I was a little nervous and worried I would screw up the process because my mind wanders so much. I thought I would have to concentrate and watch the lights without being distracted. When we first began, I was very tense in my chair as the lights started to pass back and forth. I watched and then I started to hear the therapist's words. I thought to myself, *God how do I concentrate on what she is saying when I have to watch these lights and manage all the other thoughts in my head*? As she talked I realized what she was saying and I started forgetting everything else.

She wanted me to imagine I was behind the wheel of a car. For a moment I resisted; I didn't want to be scared to death, but then I went with it. I thought about forcing myself to sit behind the steering wheel and imagined I was sitting there. My stomach began to hurt, my back started aching, my head even started hurting and my body became extremely tense. I continued to watch the lights go back and forth, noticing that they would change speed every now and again.

As I watched the lights, my counselor continued asking me questions about how I felt and what I thought was going to happen if I drove. I went through the list of bad things I knew were inevitable if I drove that car. First on the list: Larry was going to find out and beat the crap out of me. That was a real possibility I thought, and I wanted to hear her try to talk me out of being scared of that! She said some words to me that changed my life forever. "You are going to get hit no matter what, so you might as well be doing something to get hit for," she said in a matter of fact voice. I couldn't believe it – with those words, all my stress began to fall away. I continued on with my list and each excuse I came up with, she put me right in the middle of it and made me feel the anxiety. As I went through each scenario and as I watched those beautiful little lights go back and forth, the anxiety disappeared! *How quick and easy,* I thought when we were done, but would I really be able to just hop in the car and drive?

I made it home after my appointment, walked in the house and looked around. There was no sign of Larry. I looked at my children and I looked to the top of the T.V. where the keys were. I took a deep breath, grabbed the keys, picked up Alex and took Haley by the hand. I walked right out the front door, right down the steps I had sat on so many times staring at the car, opened the car door and buckled Haley and Alex into their car seats. I sat in the driver's seat, looked back at my girls, started the car, and put it in reverse. As I took my foot off the brake, I knew this was it – there was no turning back. Larry would know for sure I had taken the car out! I didn't care. I was taking my girls to get a kid's meal and I did just that. I was just a little nervous, but not enough to stop me. From that day forward, I was different I was a real person, driving like a real person, and nothing was going to stop me from doing it again.

Larry wasn't happy I had left and all hell broke loose, but surprisingly I wasn't scared. My perspective about Larry had changed completely through that experience. He didn't tower ten feet over me anymore. I wasn't small and helpless now, I was powerful. My therapist was right, I was going to get hit anyway and I might as well be getting hit for something instead of nothing. The power of feeling like a functioning person grew greater every day. The fear transformed into something I had never been – confident. I don't know if Larry knew I was different that day, and I don't really care. My mind began going to work thinking of all the things I could do with my life. I wanted to go to college and I wanted to have friends again. I wanted to go out and do things with people and live life. I wanted to have fun and live, instead of just survive.

To this day I am still amazed how one therapy session, one counselor sharing her care and expertise, jump-started my heart again. Such a small thing, such a short appointment, was the boost I needed to begin moving in the direction of living once again.

CHAPTER 6

A SHIFT

"A miracle is a shift in perception from fear to love."
[Marianne Williamson]

After just a couple of sessions with my counselor, the focus of my life shifted: I was no longer sitting around waiting or praying for something to happen, I began making things happen for myself. As I did, one thing right after another started fitting into place and it all almost made the abuse bearable. As much as I was making things happened, there are just some things we can't do on our own; and those things are called miracles. Something was about to enter my life, just when I needed it.

When you read just about how things fall into place, my story will start to grow for you as it did for me. The unexplainable things make life interesting and recognizing them is a great way to say "thank you" to whatever powers that exist which set them into motion. I can look at my story and see the words of the contract I made for myself come to life, and I can start to see how I placed each thing strategically to fit into the puzzle. It is the miracle stories that give me faith and belief in the unseen.

Miracles are delivered in numerous ways and if you keep your mind and your eyes open, you will find they are all around you. When something seems unusual to you, don't push it out of the way; hang on just a little bit, just like I did. The outcome might be something you would never have expected.

"Unexpected" was what I discovered early on a weekday morning. I was busy getting Haley ready for school when I caught sight of something through the window that faced the front yard. It was something white, fast, on all fours, and huge. I quickly ran over to the window and peeked out. It was just a stray dog. He looked as if he belonged to someone as it was apparent he had been very well cared for. He dashed back and forth through the yard as if he was looking for something. I did not pay much attention to the menace and went back to my business.

After taking care of breakfast, it was time to take Haley to school. The thought of the stray dog had almost escaped my mind. As I moved towards the door, I remembered the dog and realized I was going to have to take my kids out there. The idea of the strange dog running loose scared me a little, but I figured surely he had moved on his way. I peeked out the window again. I looked everywhere, the coast was clear and I was relieved to see the dog was gone. I scooped up Alex into my arms and carried her to the door with Haley following behind us. I opened the door and right there in front of me, as if he appeared out of thin air, was the very same ghostly-white dog. Quickly I rushed back in the house, my heart was pounding so hard I could hear it. I cracked the door open and he was still there on the step, right in front of the door. He looked up at me with his big brown eyes, as if he was saying, "You are being so rude, let me in!"

"Go on get out of here!" I yelled, just loud enough so he would know I was talking to him.

He just began to wag his long, thick tail as if he was happy that I acknowledged his existence. I figured the dog was more annoying than he was viscous, and I quickly developed a plan of action. I was going to open the door and walk to the car with Alex. Then I would get Alex in her car seat and close the car door and go back up to the house and carry Haley to the car. I would do all of this while pretending the dog was not even there. I took a deep breath, picked up Alex, and explained to Haley not to open the door once I was out. Slowly I cracked the door open and as soon as he noticed the door was opening, the nosey dog rushed right past me and jumped up on my couch, laid down and began to watch T.V.! I grabbed Haley by the arm and pulled her out of the house and quickly shut the door. I put the kids in the car and went back up to the house. I attempted to get the weirdo out of my house. Again I yelled, "Go out of here!" This time I yelled louder and more firmly than I had before, to let him know I meant business!

I stood there pointing at the door and said, "Go home. Go on, get off of my couch!"

The white dog just looked at me for a second, and then turned his eyes back to the T.V. I did not have time for his games, so I announced to him that I would deal with him when I got back, and I left and shut the door behind me. Haley's school was only a few blocks away so it did not take Alex and me long to get back home. I left Alex sitting in the car and I walked back up to the door. I opened the door to the house and there was the mysterious beast still lying on the couch. I looked at the other end of the couch and saw our dog, Thelma. There she was, lounging, as if she was on vacation. I looked at Thelma and said, "If you think he is alright, then he is alright. I guess he's OK with me."

Thelma was a very particular dog who did not like any other animals. It did not matter if it was a dog, cat or squirrel, she would go nuts. And yet, there she was lying on the couch with this dog she had just met. I trusted Thelma with my life, she rarely left my side. She had even made attempts to save me against Larry on different occasions. She was always there to listen to my troubles, and now I needed to listen to her. Somehow, in a way only she knew how, she put my mind at ease. I got Alex from the car and we went into the house.

I warned Alex not to mess with the dog as I started to contemplate what I was going to do with him. As I sat down to give myself a minute to think, Thelma and the stranger got up and went to the kitchen. They both started eating from Thelma's dog dish! I just could not believe it; Thelma was acting like this dog was her best friend! It was as if they had an unspoken language. I went the rest of the day with the dog in the house. I kind of got used to him being there and figured he was nice enough. When I let him out to go to the bathroom, he came back every time.

Larry asked around town if anyone was missing a dog, but no one knew anything about him. After a couple of days, the kids and I named him Casper. I watched the "lost and found" section in the paper every day and there was nothing to give me any clues as to where this dog had come from. Then, about two weeks later, there was an ad describing Casper right down to the very last detail. A little saddened by the idea he belonged to someone, I still called the phone number right away.

"Hello?" the lady answered.

"I am calling about the lost dog you put in the paper. I think I have your dog," I said, and then explained where I lived.

"Julie? Is that you?"

"Yes, it is. Who is this?" I said, thinking the owner was as strange as the dog.

"It's me, Mary!"

It had been about four years since Mendy, Mary and I had gotten in the fight Larry instigated, which ended our friendship. Mary and I talked for a little while on the phone, and then she came right over to pick up Casper (a.k.a., Dodo). Mary had moved only a couple of blocks away from where I lived. We joked about how, out of all the houses, her dog came to mine. "It was like he came in and made himself at home," I told Mary.

Mary and I both laughed at the idea of the pompous dog and his crazy actions. We both thought it must be some kind of sign from above and we should keep in contact. It was somewhat awkward talking after all those years, but it felt good to have a friend again. Mary left and went on with her life, and I with mine. We did not keep our promise to keep in touch.

About a month later I walked out the front door and walking up my driveway was that very same crazy, ghostly-white dog. I called Mary right away and we laughed so hard I almost cried. We both knew we had better keep in touch or else, and we have. As for the dog, it was a couple of days later he ran away again. I am sad to say he never came back and Mary was never able to find him. It was a mysterious ending for a mysterious character.

That dog had perfect timing because Mary and I needed each other. She was also having a hard time with her controlling boyfriend. Mostly we would give each other encouragement and we made each other stronger. We talked on the phone every day and became best friends. Mary and I started going out and having fun. We were a couple of free spirits when we were together. Sometimes we would take her three boys and my two girls and do kid stuff. On the weekends Haley and Alex would go to their grandma's house and Mary and I would go out and have so much fun. We went out dancing and just enjoyed doing real life things, just like normal people do. I loved being out and being myself again. Everybody loved it when we showed up because we were the life of the party.

Larry tried to cause problems with Mary and me again, but this time we were smarter and we knew what he was capable of. Her boyfriend didn't like me much either, but I didn't care. I wasn't letting my friend go, not this time.

Control, just like reality, is an illusion. If someone can create the illusion through physical smoke and foggy mirrors, such as hitting you, then they have achieved the act of control through fear tactics.

When you take anxiety and fear from the equation, the smoke begins to fade and the mirrors become clear, and you put the control back into your own hands. Through my own experience I learned as you start to gain back your control over your life, your abuser will start to feel out of control. In my case, it made the abuse much worse.

What I did in my specific situation and what I endured is not a suggestion of what anyone else should do, each and every person is different. I just tell my story as a way to get others to look back at their own lives. Through my stories I hope you can see that what I have gone through and what you are going through and what will happen, is for a purpose.

My situation could just as easily have turned out with me dead because of how I chose to deal with my abuser. Instead of leaving, I chose to stay and just take the abuse (I still had it stuck in my mind that I had nowhere to go, but a shelter and the idea of that scared me worse than staying with Larry). Many times I have written about how we create our own worlds and how we are responsible for what we go through. So if we are the creators of our own worlds, then why would I create something as horrible as being abused and controlled? It was a lesson of resilience and for me to look back on as a reminder that I don't always have to be so stubborn.

Our abusers start to become crazy as we start to gain control because they are created from the part of our subconscious mind which does not want to move on and does not want to have to be responsible for our own happiness. This resistance to allowing happiness into your life is really what is chaotic and irrational. The mind starts grasping for anything to cling to which will allow you to stay where you are at.

The biggest excuse I created for not leaving was what Larry's mom had said to me so many times about Larry's grandfather having a heart attack if I left. This rolled around and around in my head every time I thought of leaving. Her voice would replay in my mind, "It's going to kill him." Guilt can be as paralyzing as anxiety. I just couldn't be responsible for taking someone's life like that. I would tell myself it wasn't possible, but he was old and what if by chance I did leave and it did happen? Whatever excuses I gave for staying really came down to the fact that I was just plain scared. I wasn't just scared of Larry, I was scared of being alone.

It wasn't in my contract to continue being abused though. And eventually, one by one, my excuses were disappearing. The universe has a way of moving you forward to keep you on the path towards fulfilling your contract. The stronger feelings I had for an excuse and the more meaning my excuses had for me, like being responsible if Larry's grandfather died because I left, the harder the impact it had on me when it was time for me to let go of the excuse.

Sometimes the mind creates havoc to get its point across, as if it is trying to shock you into a new reality. When those old beliefs just don't fit anymore, it can be like a punch in your stomach. But, these abrupt moments are written into your contract too, as part of your experience. Larry's grandfather was old and we all knew he was sick. It is never easy when someone you love is at the end of their life, but the way it happened let me know exactly how much that excuse meant for me. Larry's grandpa had been in the hospital for surgery and had been released to go home. Since I had started driving again I found myself using any reason I could to be behind the wheel and, as much as I loved Larry's grandpa, I was happy to help him in any way I could. I had been doing errands for him, like running to the store and picking up his medicine, and I would even drive over to his house just to have meaningless conversation on his steps. As many times as I had been over to his house, I had never gone in. Larry's grandpa was a hoarder and did not allow anyone into his home. I didn't mind sitting outside chatting and I understood he was embarrassed about his problems with hoarding.

One morning after dropping Haley off at school, Alex, who was three at the time, and I headed over to pick up Grandpa's prescription and run it to the pharmacy. I pulled up in the drive way and the house looked closed and as quiet as usual. I got out of the car and unbuckled Alex from her car seat. I carried her up to the back door and we knocked as hard as we could. At first I didn't think anything of it when he didn't come to the door right away, and after a few minutes of standing there I knocked again, louder this time. A few more minutes later, I pounded on the door. My heart started to sink, but I didn't want to think the worst. It just couldn't be possible, he had to be alright. I knew he had to be sound asleep and he did have hearing problems. It wasn't unreasonable to think that he just couldn't hear us. Yet something inside me was worried. I started to panic a little and began to get more serious about getting his attention.

I started pounding on the door so hard the neighbor across the street heard me. She and her oldest son came over and before I knew it, her son had kicked the door in. Without thinking I rushed into the house not knowing where anything was, and I followed the path he had made amongst all his treasures. I ran through the narrow path to the back of the house and there he was slumped over. "Harold!" I yelled as I through my hand over Alex's eyes. I rushed out of the house as fast as I could.

Feeling like someone had sucked the breath from my body, I said, "He's in there, he's gone!"

The neighbor and her son rushed in and seconds later returned to me to confirm what I already knew. It seemed like just minutes later there were police, ambulances and the fire department there. I knew I had to be the one to find him; he wouldn't have wanted anyone else to. When I was in that moment it was as if I was standing there with the contract to my life in my hands. I knew what Harold's death meant for me.

Just a couple of days after finding Harold, I had a dream. I walked into his house and everything was clean and empty. As I walked in I noticed a picture in a gold frame up on a mantle. I was pulled into that picture and it was so warm and peaceful there. It was like sitting in the green grass on a sunny day after you have been freezing cold all winter. Harold was there and he took me by the arm. We left the picture and went back to his living room and we walked to the kitchen. There were wolves there digging through the mess on the floor. Harold let me know he didn't like the wolves digging in his things and asked me to get them out. Then we walked back to the living room and he sat in his rocking chair. He pulled up one of his shirt sleeves and he showed me his flexed muscle, and said, "I am strong again." As I looked at him I realized he was young and he was happy. He told me he was free, and then he said, "So are you." He went back into the picture with the golden frame and left me.

There were no excuses left to keep me with Larry except my own fears, inability to deal with change, and the need I had to never let people and even material things go. Since my last excuse had perished away and there was nothing physically left, I had to keep moving forward. I signed up for college and continued to rely on Mary for strength. Before long, she was moving out of her boyfriend's house, back in with her mom, and going to college too. We still hung out on the weekends; we were each other's life line.

Larry would do things like constantly say or pretend like he was going to kill himself on a daily basis. He would cut himself and call the cops on me and tell them I did it. They never believed him, so I didn't get in trouble. Although I logically knew Larry was mentally ill and it was not because of me and things I was doing, I still stayed. Now, even though Harold was gone, I just kept coming up with excuse after excuse.

I didn't want to leave my house and all my things again, like I had done when my mom died. I was still scared to be on my own and be alone as some fears are a lot harder than others to overcome. Plus if I had contact with Larry, I felt as if I could tell day-by-day what he was thinking and feeling. Somehow knowing what mood he was in made me feel safer. When you live with someone with a mental disorder you understand it feels safer to know what mood they are in than sit around wondering what they are thinking. At least I knew if he was crazy enough to kill me, it wouldn't be a sneak attack; rather, it would probably be at home and I might have a chance to get away.

The things you tell yourself to continue to stay comfortable and stuck are just as crazy as the person you are allowing to hurt you every day. When you are living with someone who has a mental illness it wears you out and unless you have deep love for that person, you can't and don't want to understand why they are the way they are. But by not paying attention you are ignoring the part of you that brought them into your life.

I made attempts to leave a couple of times. Larry would threaten me with kidnapping Haley and Alex. He would tell me, "I am going to take them and you will never see them again." I was scared to lose my girls and scared that he might get desperate enough to hurt them to get back at me, so I would come back. I tried going to the police, but they would tell me, "He is their father and there is nothing we can do if he wants to take them."

I was mentally done with the relationship and I think if Larry had been in his right mind, he would have admitted to being done too. As much as he wanted me to be there he had already been seeing other women and I knew it. I needed more support to get through this and I could feel the storm coming. It was as if it had been announced on T.V. Unbeknownst to me, things started building in my life in preparation for what was about to happen.

One day when I was with Mary she talked me into seeing Mendy again. I had not seen her for 5 years since we had all had the big fight because of Larry's lies. I missed her, but wasn't sure if she wanted to see me. I told Mary I didn't want to go because there were a lot of hurt feelings. Mendy had no idea she had been lied to and thought I had really said horrible things about her. Mendy didn't know Larry was so controlling and was on a mission to destroy our relationship back then. She wasn't welcoming me with open arms, but after some talking and putting together the truth, and me admitting to my childhood friend I was being abused, we made up. Now I had my best friend back and life was getting even better.

One day, shortly after making up with Mendy, we were hanging out at her house when I met my knight in shining armor. Andy was different than any man I had ever met. He was smart, had a job, a house and was fun to be around. He was worried about me and my kids and wanted to help, yet somehow he was understanding about why I couldn't leave just yet. I didn't have to be afraid knowing he was in my life. He seemed to know what to do with any problem or situation that came up. Even with Andy, Mendy and Mary on my side, I was still terrified of Larry taking Haley and Alex from me. My worst fear was Larry would just go to the school, pick the girls up, and I would never see them again. I told the school of my concerns about Larry and they said the same as the police, "He is their father, we have to let him take them."

Yet they had never seen him, not even once. They had no idea what the girls' dad looked like. They promised me they would notify me if anyone tried to pick them up. Terrified, I knew something big was going to have to happen to make me leave and make me stay gone.

CHAPTER 7

LESSONS

"Hard times don't create heroes. It is during the hard times when the hero within us is revealed." [Bob Riley]

I reached the conclusion that two things needed to happen for me to leave Larry. The first was I needed to be thrown into a reality where I recognized the illusion in which I was living, and I'll get to the second momentarily.

Larry owned everything, he was still in control, but I thought of everything as mine too. And just like the situation with my Mom, Larry had the option to take everything from me whenever he wanted. He was about to prove he still had control over me and I was a fool to think that by staying, I was never in control of anything. I am so grateful to coming to this conclusion and appreciate it was Larry that gave me this lesson. Like most people, I learn lessons the hard way. The more resistant we are, the deeper the root of the belief we need to be taught to overcome, and the more meaningful the lesson.

It was the night before my first final exams. I had put Haley and Alex to bed and continued to study. Being obsessed with my grades and a horrible test taker, I was nervous about finals. It was around midnight when Larry came out of his room and decided he wanted to talk to me. I said, "Not right now, I have a test tomorrow and I need to study."

He continued to talk. I ignored him as I fell deeper into study mode. He became louder and louder the more I ignored him. I got up and walked to the kitchen and continued to study. Of course he followed me and before I knew it he was coming at me. By chance the phone rang and I quickly picked up the receiver. "Hello?" I said, slightly out of breath from battling with Larry. "What's wrong?" a voice on the other end said. Realizing it was Mary on the other end I blurted out, "He's at it again."

Larry stopped pestering momentarily until he realized it was Mary I was talking to. Hearing him in the background Mary said, "Hang up and call the cops."

"No. I can't," I whispered into the phone.

I don't know why I couldn't; for some reason I was scared of calling the cops. I guess maybe I didn't want to be someone who couldn't handle myself and I was scared of what Larry would do once the cops left.

Mary began trying to convince me to call the police, but before I knew it the phone went dead. I looked over and Larry had unplugged it from the wall. He was furious that I had the time to talk to Mary, but not to him. He began to yell at me to talk to him. I yelled back "No, just leave me alone."

It probably would have been safer for me to just talk to Larry, but all he wanted to do was belittle me with his words and keep me from studying so I would fail my test. I knew what he was doing and what he meant by "talk to me." To be honest, by that point the very idea of sitting there looking at Larry made me sick to my stomach. By this time it was about two in the morning and I was ready for bed. I finally told Larry, "I am just going to go to bed. I am tired and I have school tomorrow."

"No you're not!" he said, in a rotten sort of way.

I didn't want him following me into the bedroom where Haley and

Alex were, so I laid down on the couch and closed my eyes. He just kept talking and telling me how stupid I was. He kept telling me I was going to fail my test and I would never finish college so I should just quit. With every word he spoke I wished he would go further and further away from me.

I started to silently pray in my head, asking God to make him stop. As soon as I did there was a knock on the door. My first thought was Mary had come to see if I was okay since Larry wouldn't let me call her back. I jumped up and answered the door. There were two officers standing there on the front step. "We received a call you were having some troubles," one of the cops said.

I walked outside and Larry stayed in the house. Mary had called the cops because she was worried about me, I felt certain. One cop took me out into the yard and one asked Larry to come talk to him. As I stood in the wet grass explaining to the cop exactly what I had been dealing with that night and even told him Larry had a tendency to get violent, I thought they would protect me. When the officer was done hearing what I had to say, he and his partner spoke silently as they decided what to do with the situation.

After a couple of minutes I was told to go stand by Larry so they could talk to us. As the words began to pour from their mouth, my heart sank as I realized what they were telling me. "You have to stay up and talk to him or leave," said the officer I was not familiar with. I looked in a puzzled way towards the cop I thought was on my side. "He owns the house and he can make you leave, will you agree to stay up and talk to him?" he said.

"I have kids sleeping in the house! You seriously are not going to make me wake my kids up and leave are you?" I asked in my defense.

"Yes, you will have to leave if you don't agree to talk to him."

Disgusted, I agreed to stay up and talk to Larry as was requested of me, and I walked back into the house. Larry followed me as the cops got into their cars and drove away. He said, "Now you have to talk to me."

I looked at him deliberately, being obtuse with my attitude. Without saying a word, I laid down on the couch, closed my eyes and began to contemplate what happened. Larry didn't do anything to me that night or make me leave, but it was fuel to add to his fire and as he grew angrier day by day, it was just a matter of time before he blew up. This moment was the first ingredient I needed for my realization recipe.

The second element was about to happen and it was a realization that I had about myself. The moment when you are faced with a decision that you can't turn back from is the moment you realize exactly who you are. It has nothing to do with the decision itself, but the reason behind why you did what you did that counts. Love drives most of us and passion makes us strong enough to overcome fears; fears are the obstacle to making the right decision in most cases, the decision we know to be the best course. When you put love and passion together it makes us like superheroes, invincible in that time and space even if just for a second. A superhero will purposely put themselves in harm's way just to save an innocent. They do it without worry about how they will feel or what will happen to them. They just rush in without any limited beliefs.

I wouldn't ever call myself a superhero, but just maybe I felt like one the day I left Larry. It had been a long day, but a happy one. I had received my student loan and was excited to get my new books for the next semester's classes. This was during a time when we still had paper checks to cash, and that one little piece of paper was about to set off a string of events that led me to see my way out. I had been out that day and gotten the check earlier, when I was in a hurry. I had detached it from the stub and put it back in the envelope and placed it in my purse. When I got home, before I even gotten out of the car, I remembered I placed it there and I took it out just for a moment to

FINDING THE ROAD TO REASON

stare at it. Once I was done I placed it carefully back in the safety of my purse, got Haley and Alex out of the car and locked the purse and the check in my car. With a smile on my face I walked up to the house and went in.

I was met with an angry, downright bitter Larry who, while I was out that day, found the stub to my student loan. I had no idea why he was mad and I didn't care. I tried to ignore his efforts to involve me in his world of craziness. Then he said, "Where is it?" Knowing what he meant I still asked, "Where is what?"

"Where is the check from your student loan? Give it to me."

"No!" I screamed back at him. Haley and Alex quickly ran to our bedroom because they knew what was going to happen. He came at me fast and tried to scare me into telling him where the check was. I refused to tell him. Frantically he ran back and forth through the house as he stopping here and there to look through places he knew I usually kept my papers. Then, like a light bulb went off in his head, he turned and looked at me and said, "It's in your purse, isn't it?"

"No!" I yelled, in a tone of voice he knew meant I was lying. He rushed out the front door and to the car. I could hear him trying to open the locked door. I felt like my life would be over if he found my check. I remember I had the keys to the car in my pocket and if he couldn't find them that would buy me some time. Quickly I thought of places where I could hide the keys. Before I had time to think, he was back in my face screaming for me to give him the keys.

Those precious keys were still tucked in the pocket of my jacket. For just a second I looked into Larry's eyes and I saw evil, something I had never seen in his eyes before. I was scared, I panicked like a claustrophobic being buried six feet deep. All the strength I had ever prayed for came to me in this moment and somehow I was able to work myself free of his grasp. All I could think about were Haley and

Alex, I had to get to my girls. My instinct led me to the bedroom door. Somehow, even though I had gotten away, Larry was right behind me. I tried to slam the door shut as fast and hard as I could, but he was right there. He pinned me in the corner right by the door, blocking it so Haley and Alex couldn't leave. He punch me in the jaw, I dropped to the ground, crouched with my hands over my head trying to protect myself from his violent kicks. All of a sudden I felt nothing. My attention was drawn to a new pain. It was a pain in my heart I can't ever find the words to explain.

I looked at my little girls sitting on the bed watching. With no expression and no tears, they observed as their mother was getting abused. All of a sudden I knew I wasn't the victim anymore, they were. They were numb to the chaos that was going on right in front of them. What I was allowing to happen to them was horrible.

No little girl should ever see their mother getting hit and beaten and my girls had watched it so much it had become normal to them. The love and the passion I had that day drove me up from the ground. Although I am only five-foot-two and Larry is six-foot-one, somehow I was face to face with the evil I had run from for way too long. From the very deepest depth of my lungs I commanded, "No More, you are done."

That one declaration stunned Larry enough to stop hitting me, it was as if I had stopped time and he was frozen in the moment. I pushed him out of my way, grabbed my little girls - each one by the arm - and we walked out of the house to the car. Without contemplation of anything at all, I took those precious keys out of my pocket and we drove away. I took my girls to Cindy's house and assuring them I was fine, I promised them I would be back. I went to the hospital and because of all the bruises and the broken tooth, the hospital called the police. Larry was arrested, but only held for a short time. A restraining order was placed against him and he was ordered to take classes to help him with his anger issues. Of course, he did ask me to pay for them.

Shortly after that day, I went to pick up Haley and Alex from school and they weren't there. My worst nightmare had come true. During the day Larry had gone and picked them up and the school never called me! I was frantic, I knew I couldn't go over to his house to get them because of the restraining order. The only person I could think of that would know what to do was Andy. I went to him right away. He took me to the police station and he explained my situation. They told him to take me to Larry's house and they would met us there. It only took us a few minutes before we were parked out in front of my old house. The officer got out and told me the only way I could get my girls back was if Larry let them leave the house and they came out to me. He said, "If you are lucky enough, he will let them go; once they are with you, put them in the car and drive away."

I was scared to think what Larry would do if he was able to keep them. Didn't my kids have a right to be with their own mother? How could he be allowed to keep them trapped in that house?

I wasn't allowed to walk up to the door. As the cop did, I saw the door open slowly. As quick as lightening, I saw Haley push her way past Larry with Alex right behind her. It was as if they read my mind. I opened my arms as wide as I could and I yelled, "Come here, come to me!" Within seconds my little girls were in the car and Andy and I were driving away with them. I was so happy I knew they were back with me and they were safe. I am not sure why Larry never tried to take them from school again, but he didn't. I faced my fear of Larry taking the only thing that kept me going in this world, I wasn't afraid anymore. I knew my girls loved me and I knew no one could change that.

I lived with my sister for a short time and then Andy offered for the kids and me to come live with him. I was excited to move forward with Andy and start a new life. School was going well and I had a new job working as a maid in a hotel. Haley and Alex seemed happier too now that they didn't have to deal with all the fighting. I was a little sad when my counselor informed me I didn't need her anymore, but I knew I was going to be okay and I could final say that life was great! I worked hard in school and eventually I worked my way up to eight classes in one semester, and still worked and took care of my share of the bills.

Before I knew it I was also doing an internship at our local humane society. Even though I wasn't getting paid, I worked hard and when I graduated they asked me to come work there full-time as a veterinary technician. I had never been more proud of myself.

Hard work and keeping busy was just a substitution for the misery I kept hiding inside. Things were great on the outside and I learned to act like I was happy; sometimes I even was, but it seemed the harder I worked and more I didn't need Andy to be my savior, the less he wanted me. I felt like more of a trophy he had saved out of the trash. Yet that wasn't the reason for my depression. I was still feeling sorry for myself. I was in a constant state of self-loathing if I wasn't working.

Being depressed is like standing in the middle of a garden full of blossoming roses, everyone around you can see their beauty and you even know it is there, but your senses are so sensitive that all you can smell is the fertilizer they grow in. It really isn't a "mind over matter" issue; no matter how much you tell yourself you should see those roses and their beauty, you just don't care and appreciate it like you should. My perspective was stuck on being life's victim.

I had no other perspective to base my life on – I just kept waiting for the next bad thing to happen. I could barely remember what life was like before Mom died and even before then, life wasn't really the most ideal. It wasn't that I was sad every day and walked around moping, but it was the silent moments that tore me up. I loved taking care of the animals at the shelter and I was good at it and I was still good at being a mom and I started to get comfortable in my life. Then after being with Andy for a couple of years, I found out I was pregnant. I was very excited about the news and for the first time I thought for sure I was doing this thing called life like everyone else. During my pregnancy I thought for sure Andy was going to be excited and he seemed to be, for the most part. This was his first child, Andy was ten years older than me and this was his first baby!

Each time we would tell his friends we were having a baby they would be in shock at first, then almost sympathetic. I thought it was an odd way to react to two people in love, having a baby, until one day one of Andy's friends, who just happened to be his ex-girl's sister, said, "You know Andy wasn't meant to be a dad. Everyone knows this except you. Don't you ever wonder why no one is excited for you guys? Everyone is just shocked after what happened with my sister."

The horrified look on my face must have made her feel the need to explain what she meant. "My sister had been pregnant many times and each time Andy talked her into an abortion, he will talk you into one too."

"Oh no he won't!" I yelled. "That can't be true, he is good to Haley and Alex."

"Ask him about it," she said, in a cocky kind of way. "Haley and Alex aren't babies and they go to their grandma's on the weekend. Wait until you have a baby who can't just pick up and go all the time. You guys are pretty much over."

With that idea in my head I stewed about it for a little while, but thought surely he could change. Was it even true about his ex-girlfriend? I had to find out. I worked up the nerve and asked him about what I had heard.

"Yes, it's true," he said. Then he explained to me why he had talked her into the abortions. "She was using drugs and drinking, the babies would have never made it."

"Then why would you continue to be careless and get her pregnant?" I asked.

He was silent and just looked at me like I was being ridiculous. I was angry, this man who I thought was my noble savior was nothing more than someone who went around saving damsels in distress. I saw him in a completely different way then. I wasn't the first woman who he thought needed his saving. He had done this before and then got some sort of sick fix off of being better than them.

"Do not ever ask me to get an abortion. Do you understand me?" I said. He just walked out of the room without saying a word or even looking at me. I felt lost again and alone.

I was happy about having my baby and Andy played along too. He went to doctor appointments once in a while and seemed to care. I didn't like my doctor much; he was just a resident and every time I felt like something was wrong, he would act like I was over-reacting. Andy, at least, felt sorry for me that the doctor didn't listen. In my doctor's defense I did always worry too much. I thought at one point about getting a different doctor. I even told Andy, "I just don't like Dr. Pranger and I don't think he likes me." For some reason Andy talked me out of it.

In my defense I was pregnant and I was really sick to my stomach a lot. I was sick so much it wasn't long until people at work started getting suspicious. I never even missed work despite being sick. I still loved my job; I still chased down runaway dogs and dealt with the emotions of having to euthanize whatever I was told to, even the puppies. I was about three months along when I went in and told my boss about my fun and exciting news. A few days later I was let go. Now with no job and a baby on the way, I had to make my savings and unemployment last. I tried hard to get a job, but no one was hiring and the further along I got in in my pregnancy, it looked even more impossible. The longer I went without a job the more frustrated Andy became and he started to make me feel like a loser.

I started to realize exactly whose responsibility this baby was and – mine and mine alone! As long as my share of the bills were paid, I knew I would be okay.

On May 17th, 2002, I dropped Haley and Alex off at school, went home and was just feeling exhausted from a horrible night's sleep. I was very close to my due date and had had false contractions all night. I sat down in the rocking chair, turned on the T.V. and began to watch one of my favorite shows, "Little House on the Prairie," just to take my mind off of everything. I started rocking back and forth as I watched Pa share his wisdom around Walnut Grove. Then, before I even knew what had happened, I felt what could only be described as a balloon popping inside my stomach. I quickly stood up and I was soaking wet! My water had broken! When it happened with my other children I was in the hospital, so I didn't know what to do. I went and woke Andy up and called the hospital. Andy was moving slowly. He had to take a shower, then when he was done with that he had to stop and get coffee. By the time we made it to the maternity ward, I was soaking wet from my bottom down to my socks.

I was quickly admitted and Dr. Pranger came into my room shortly after with a big smile on his face. "Are you sure your water broke?" he asked.

A little annoyed, I started to open my mouth when a nurse said, "There is no doubt her water broke!" She looked at me with a smile on her face as if to say, "I got your back, girl."

Dr. Pranger was in his excited mode and told me he was taking a culture, to make sure. Moments later he came back and confirmed what we all knew already, my water broke and I was about to have my baby. I couldn't wait for another baby girl to take care of and love.

It was just a couple of pushes and there was this beautiful tiny five pound little bundle of boy! That's right, a little boy! The ultrasound said it was a girl, but he was a wonderful boy. I couldn't believe it, or maybe I could because even though I had been told I was having a girl, I somehow knew not to buy girl stuff. I had bought everything neutral. Deep down inside I think I had always known it was going to be a boy. I had even picked out a boy name. Andy didn't worry about what we would name it if it was a boy, so he told me go ahead and name him what I wanted and I did. Griffith Andrew named after the best man ever to exist, Andy Griffith. I grew up watching him on T.V., daydreaming that someday I could have my own Andy Griffith, and now I did! No matter what name I had given him, I felt so connected with my little guy even before I held him in my arms. Then once he was in my arms, I never wanted to put him down.

I felt Griffin was my reward for finding the courage to leave Larry and for standing up to Andy. I was becoming my own person, and Griffin's birth was a celebration of that fact.

CHAPTER 8

FINDING SELF-CONFIDENCE

"Our self-respect tracks our choices. Every time we act in harmony with our authentic self and our heart, we earn our respect. It is that simple. Every choice matters." [Dan Coppersmith]

It didn't take long for me to be discharged and then it was time to go home from the hospital with my Griffie. I was relieved to be headed back home so I could take care of normal life things, like getting the kids to school and getting used to having a baby around again. Plus, while in the maternity ward I had picked up a really bad head cold. My sinuses felt like they were on fire and blowing my nose became a never-ending task. I just wanted to be home in my bed.

My thoughts began to wander on the ride home and I found myself thinking about how long it had been since I had a little baby to take care of. Alex was seven now and Haley was ten, so it had been awhile; but I wasn't worried at all about falling right back into the role of mommy again. My serene thoughts of enjoying my new baby were cut short by Andy. "You know some women go back to work the day after they have their baby," he said.

Knowing exactly what he was getting at I said, "Good for them, too bad for their baby though."

I don't know if Andy replied to my smart ass comment because I stopped paying attention as we pulled up to the side of the house. The car was barely stopped before I jumped out. I couldn't wait to hold my baby again! I got Grif's car seat and walked as quickly as I could across the yard and into the house. Once in the house I placed the car seat next to the chair and I sat down. Grif was sleeping so I left him for the moment. Andy had come in behind me and started talking again about me getting a job. I closed my eyes and pretended I didn't hear him, and finally he shut up.

I sat there in the chair with my eyes closed for however long Grif would allow me to. Haley and Alex had been at their grandma's house and were on their way home. I couldn't wait to be with all my children in one place. As happy as I was, my joy was shadowed by the stupid cold I had picked up. It seemed it kept getting stronger by the minute, and I was getting weaker. I just hoped Griffie didn't get it, he was so tiny.

Haley and Alex arrived home and we were all together. I felt a peace in my heart that made me know things were okay and complete, for now. I just wanted to be a mom and take care of my kids. I still had some savings so money wasn't a worry for me at the moment, though Andy seemed to become increasingly worried and the little conversations turned into long drawn out battles. He was convinced I was lazy. I just had a baby and was sick, and I didn't feel much like continuing to look for jobs when I had been doing it for the last six months. I also didn't want to leave my baby with someone and go off to work.

I went to the doctor for my sickness, which had obviously turned into some type of infection, because it was not getting any better. Not only did it not get better, this sickness sucked every bit of energy I had. The constant fever, the coughing and the congestion were so bad and I had tried every kind of cold medicine I could get my hands on. The antibiotic the doctor gave me wasn't helping either. It was so much agony I even tried getting sympathy from Andy, but he just thought I was over reacting so I wouldn't have to get a job.

I began to feel as if I didn't get a job that very second, he was going to throw me right out the door. He became so focused on his need for me to have a job and be able to cover my share of the bills, which included everything Haley, Alex and Grif needed. Of course Larry wouldn't pay child support either, even though it was set at a whole $30/month. I kept pleading with Andy to understand how sick I was, but he just ignored me and kept hounding me about having a job.

When Grif was ten days old, I reached a breaking point. My body had had enough and it gave up. It was the weekend and the girls went to their grandma's house. It was just Andy, Grif and I. I had slept on the couch the night before, trying to find some kind of comfort so I could sleep. I didn't sleep much the night before, but somehow that night on the couch I managed to doze off. The lack of being able to breathe brought me from my state of half slumber. It felt as if someone had put a plastic bag over my mouth and nose. I lay on the couch in tears hoping Grif, who laid silently asleep in his bassinet at the end of the couch, would not wake up anytime soon. I could not get up, the pain in my chest was sharp and pinching and my back ached. I tried to yell for Andy who was sleeping in the bedroom. I opened my mouth and tried to suck in the harsh, thick air, but I could not get enough air in to yell.

As I laid on the couch as motionless as I possibly could, I started to panic in my thoughts, and the first thing I thought of was my mother. Was this how Mom had felt all the time she was sick with lung cancer? I was shocked back into reality when Grif began to wake up. I knew I had to take care of him. Despite the pain that had spread through my entire chest and back, I rolled off the couch, but then landed on the floor. I did not think I was going to be able to pull myself up from the floor. I stayed on the floor for a minute in hopes Grif would start crying harder and wake Andy. It didn't matter how hard Grif cried, Andy was used to me tending to him and wasn't going to wake up. I managed to use the coffee table as a crutch and push myself to standing. Standing hurt so badly, but once I was upright and got over to Grif, the pain started to ease just a little. I wiped my tears away and went to pick Grif up from his bassinet.

The pain of bending over made me feel like stabbing knives were sitting in my lungs. The tears came again. I walked in slow motion back to the bedroom as I gasped for air. I laid Grif in his crib. He lay there quite as if he knew something was wrong. I turned and walked the excruciating three steps to the bed where Andy lay sleeping. Doing the best I could, I shook Andy to wake up. "I need to go to the hospital," I said. It took every bit of what life I had left in me just to say those words. Andy just said, "Alright," but he never bothered to wake up. I did not have time for Andy's lack of urgency and nonchalant attitude. I knew I would have to take myself. I was running off of pure fear now and I certainly wasn't thinking straight. I was terrified I was going to die! I got Grif ready and drove myself to the hospital. I was so scared I was going to pass out while driving. I just kept thinking in my mind, *I have the baby with me, I have to make it to the hospital.*

When I arrived at the hospital I felt relief. I thought for some reason because I was at the hospital they could make me better. Although the nurses had been very sympathetic and were helping me take care of Grif, the E.R. doctor didn't make me feel better at all. He just told me that the x-rays they took showed I had pneumonia. I was given another, stronger antibiotic to take and some painkillers, then sent home. The doctor said, "I would keep you here, but you can just go home since you have your baby with you."

I was supposed to stop and get my prescriptions, but I drove myself back home instead as the feeling of suffocation was ten times worse than before. I could feel every inch of each one of my lungs. What had once felt like sharp knives now felt like heavy jagged pieces of glass. I carried Grif into the house. Now instead of feeling like I was going to die I was wanting, no begging, for it to happen.

I decided to take a bath to try to make some of the pain go away. The steam from the bath wrapped around like a warm, wet, heavy blanket after someone had pulled a plastic bag over my face. I got out of my bath, got dressed the best I could, and I stumbled to the bedroom.

I checked on Grif who was now sleeping in his crib. The wheezing from my lungs woke him. I picked him up and lay down with him in my bed.

I had Grif cradled in my arm next to me. I laid there and prayed to God in my head, begging for Him to make all the pain go away. I did not even notice Andy was not in the bed sleeping any more. As I lay there in bed, I held my breath. The pain was almost gone! I had the brilliant idea that if I didn't breathe or move I would be fine. Suffocation did not scare me anymore, as long as I didn't have to feel the pain I just didn't care if I lived or died. Images of my kids flashed in my mind -- my baby boy who was lying next to me and my girls needed me to be their mommy. I took small almost nonexistent breaths, just enough to keep me alive. Soon Andy came into the bedroom and saw me laying there.

Andy called his mother because he did not know what to do. Before I knew it his mom was standing over my bed with a concerned looked on her face. They urged me to go back to the hospital, but I told them, "I have already been to the hospital. They sent me home."

After a little more coaxing from Andy and his mother I decided it was time to go back. By the time we arrived to the hospital the shallow breaths I took were still just enough to keep me alive, but not conscious.

I woke in the hospital days later and I was even a year older since my birthday had come and gone! I recalled very little, but did remember waking up briefly in the emergency room from being poked by a needle on the inside of my wrist. It was just for a second, then I was being pulled back into the darkness. I was told later on the doctors didn't think I would make it. I was also told when I was wheeled into the E.R. with Grif in his car seat on my lap; my fingers were so tight around the handle they had to pry them off. On the inside I was laughing at the idea that even in an unconscious state I refused to let someone else take over.

After I was able to go home I felt sorry for myself. No one had cared enough to take care of me. No one knew how much pain I had been in. I vowed then and there I would take care of me and I would never let myself get that sick again. I knew I was the one who allowed no one to care for me, but it still hurt. Andy, who always made it a point to tell anyone and everybody who would listen how much he loved me, really only loved me when it was not a bother or if I had a job. Or, he loved me when things got so bad I almost died. I felt differently towards him now. I was alone again, abandoned by one more person.

I recovered from being sick finally and decided I would take my time getting a job. If Andy didn't like it, I just didn't care anymore. I looked for jobs and applied at a lot of places, but I didn't stress over it anymore. I started getting the idea it didn't matter if I had a college degree or not, the only place I was going to be able to get a job was going to pay me minimum wage, which would barely cover daycare, let alone pay my bills. Then, when Grif was about four months old, I got a job as a quality assurance inspector at a meat packing plant. I hated that job with a passion. The sound of pigs squealing as I walked in to work every night was enough to make you go crazy. The rancid smells that came from dead hogs which had carelessly been thrown next to the building would make my stomach turn as I walked across the parking lot each night.

I was working third shift so I could be there to take the kids to school and pick them up. I also needed to be there for Grif during the day. Plus it was a good job because they were willing to hire me at twelve dollars an hour, which was more than minimum wage at least.

Andy wanted me to work, but he did not want to help me with the kids. Our deal was that since he now worked first shift he would watch Grif after he got off work so I could sleep. It did not work that way at all. I would come home from work around 6:30 A.M. Andy had the kids all night while they slept. Lucky for him, Grif was sleeping through the night already. Andy only watched the kids the first couple of nights after that; I had to find a babysitter. I can't remember what Andy's excuse was for not being at home while I was working, but that was just how it was. Whatever the excuse, it was my responsibility to find someone to watch the kids so I could work. Andy was never one to let something like a baby dictate what he was doing or when he could do it.

When I came home at 6:30 A.M. I had to get the girls ready for school. Then I had to take them to school at 8:30 A.M. and then I had to stay up all day with Grif. I don't sleep well and never have, so to nap when Grif did was impossible. Andy was supposed to come home at 4:00 P.M. After I picked Haley and Alex up from school at 3:35 PM, I was supposed to come home and go to bed while he watched the kids. It never happened that way. Day after day, I would go to work with no sleep. I was able to sleep on the weekends if I didn't have to work, but it just wasn't enough. Whenever I would get discouraged, I would remind myself of the days when I was with Larry and spent countless hours on the steps outside looking at a car I thought I would never drive. I would think to myself, *you are missing something! There has to be more than this!* At least I wasn't that girl that was trapped, but being a slave for someone else to make a little over twelve dollars and hour just didn't seem like it was what I was meant to do with my life. My depression continued to linger because I didn't like going to work and leaving my kids. It wasn't that I didn't like hard work, I actually enjoy it sometimes. None of it ever felt right to me.

Despite the never ending harassment from most of the male supervisors, the only enjoyment I got from my job was the people I was working with. Most of them could barely speak any English and it was hard to communicate, but somehow we found our way to make each other laugh and we had fun. None of them wanted to be there either, but somehow they all found a way to be content with what they were doing.

There was one employee that was different, he actually grew up in Iowa just like me. He was a younger man, seven years younger than me to be exact. His name was Russell and he was very shy and did not talk to many people. Something drove Russell to talk to me though. The first time he talked to me I let him know right from the start, "I am 26, I have a boyfriend, three kids and I am tired so don't even try it."

He replied, "I don't care." He just wanted to show me some of his drawings. He was a talented artist. I am sure his artwork was a way of breaking his shyness and working up the guts to talk to someone. We became friends instantly, since I loved to draw too. I had not drawn for a long time, but I did appreciate the work and energy he had to have put into his art.

I wasn't sure exactly what Russell's motives were, but he seemed innocent enough. If he ever tried anything, I knew I could take him; he only weighed about 125 pounds! We started hanging out during the day, going shopping together, and he helped me with Grif. It was almost like having a personal assistant. All Russell wanted was to be around someone and for me it was a relief to have someone to hang out with. I never kept Russell a secret from anyone, including Andy, and made it clear that Russell and I were friends. If anyone one should have understood it would be Andy, since he had lectured me so many times about how he was entitled to have friends who were women. Andy did have a problem with it though, when I was the one with a friend of the opposite sex.

I knew everyone thought that we were having an affair, but I was too tired to care what everyone thought. I enjoyed the company and we were becoming best friends. Russell actually wanted to be around, while Andy's only concern was what he could do to be away. Russell was spending more time in one day with Grif than Andy spent with him in a week. He would even buy him the things he needed, like diapers or formula. Russell loved Grif and he hated being away from him. Although I thought Russell was great around Grif, I just I still didn't want to put my responsibility on him. He would offer to watch Grif so I could sleep once in a while, but even if I taken him up on this and tried to sleep, there was no way I could sleep during the day knowing someone else was taking care of my baby.

It was not too long before I got sick again. I pushed myself too far and I knew I would end up back at the hospital with pneumonia if I did not stop. I was going to work with a high fever, I lost my voice and my supervisor kept making me work in the freezer. He never liked me for whatever reason, probably because I didn't put up with his crap and unlike the others, I spoke excellent English. The quality assurance inspectors were supposed to take turns working in the freezer, yet night after night, I was the one sent in to freeze, sick or not.

Despite feeling like a loser, I quit working at the meat packing plant. I just could not take it any longer. I had to get some sleep. As expected, that was the straw that broke the camel's back for Andy. I didn't have job again and now he was suspicious of Russell and I. His behavior became stranger and stranger, though he was home even less than before and never gave an explanation for where he was. All of a sudden he started to lose a lot of weight, and became extremely paranoid. I thought maybe he was stressed about Russell coming around and I told Russell maybe we shouldn't hang out as much. This had an adverse effect on the situation as Andy started to think we were sneaking around now. Andy became paranoid and preoccupied with catching us doing something bad. His actions were just causing us to become closer friends.

Andy decided enough was enough, or in other words, his paranoia got the best of him. In one act, he ended what little respect I had for him. He tapped the home phone. One little thing he didn't know was that when a landline is tapped or at least the tap he was using, it makes a slight clicking sound. I had noticed it while talking to my sister, Cindy, on the phone. Maybe this sound had gone unnoticed to Andy, but to someone with my sensitive ears, I picked up on it immediately. I picked up the phone and saw an unusual cord attached to it. I followed the cord from the back of the phone to a hole in the floor. My heart sank, this was like something from a spy movie! I quickly got up, ran downstairs, and looked everywhere for a cord that looked like one that was attached to the phone. Thinking hard about where the hole was in the floor, I went into Andy's fishing room and there it was – a small tape recorder sitting on the counter. There was the wire and there was the hole in the floor.

I pressed rewind on the recorder and played the tape that was already in there. First I heard Andy's voice, then I heard his stepdad. They were going back and forth talking until they made sure the tape was picking up the phone conversation. These people who had accepted me and my kids were now all plotting against me to catch me doing something I wasn't even doing.

I thought to myself, *how dare Andy tape my phone conversations*! Not only is it just wrong, it is illegal in the state of Iowa to record telephone conversations without at least one person's consent. I probably shouldn't have, but I felt so betrayed and violated I came up with a plan to drive him nuts!

The very first thing I did was write a note to myself on a piece of paper that said what date I found the recorder. I placed the paper in a sealed envelope and I took it to the post office and had it sent to myself. The post mark on the sealed envelope would be undebatable proof of when I knew the phone was tapped. I needed this because I was about to do something so drastic, I would need evidence that I was not lying.

Because this was before cell phones were so common, I went to the gas station and called everyone I knew. I explained the phone was tapped and unless they wanted to be recorded, to not call me. The last person I called was Russell. "Andy has my phone tapped trying to catch us having an affair. I need your help."

"What can I do?" he asked.

"We are going to lay it on thick and make it seem like we are having an affair," I explained.

Russell was on board and he thought it was funny. "I just hope he don't kill us," I said, and hung up the phone.

By the time I got home Andy was there. I was sure he had the tape that I had listened too. I wanted to irritate him a little so when he said he had to go and began to leave, I stopped him.

"Where are you going"? I asked.

"Just to the store," he said.

"I need to go too!" I blurted out.

"You don't want to drag Grif out," he replied.

He often used Grif as an excuse to not allow me to go with him, but not his time. "I already have him in his car seat," I told him. So I put Grif into Andy's car and off we went to the store. Just right down the road was the gas station I had just been at calling everyone. Andy stopped. "I don't need to go to the store actually; I am just going to the gas station," he said, as if he was irritated.

Once we stopped and Andy went in to the gas station, I quickly reached under his seat and there it was, the tape that had been in the tape recorder. I felt myself smiling, knowing that I had ruined his plan to go listen to the tape. I made things just a little bit more difficult for him that day. He got back in the car and drove home. As soon as we got there, he acted like he was coming in the house and once I got Grif out of his car seat, he said he had to go somewhere else. I didn't say a word, I just smiled again, knowing what he was going to do. When he came back, he seemed a little calmer and I knew it was because there was nothing on the tape. It would not last though, Andy's world was about to be turned upside down.

Maybe Russell's and my actions weren't justified, but at the time it felt right. The next day we started laying it on hot and heavy. We were giving Andy exactly what he wanted and I watched as he became a maniac trying to hide what he was doing. He was going crazy and I was enjoying every minute of it.

I let the prank go on for about a week, then I had to let Andy in on what I had known. It was really for my own sanity that I finally told him since day-after-day and tape-after-tape the dirty looks and mean attitude became harder and harder to deal with. I knew I wasn't going to be able to trust Andy again and I knew he didn't trust me. The relationship was over.

Andy was sitting in his chair in the back yard stewing as he had done day after day. I walked out and knew telling him was going to feel good. As I began to speak, a look of relief came over his face. I told him that I had a post-marked letter of when I knew and that Russell and I staged every conversation. I walked into the house went down stairs and grabbed that stupid little recorder took it out to show him I knew where it was. I smashed that sucker on the ground as hard as I could in victory. He was so happy he just keep smiling and telling me how relieved he was. I wasn't though; I had been betrayed and treated like a criminal.

Andy tried to explain to me that people like Russell, my sister and my friends were not people I should associate myself with. He said, "I am up here." Then he took his hand and used it as a measurement, holding it way above his head. "Everyone else is down here," he said as he lowered his hand as far down as it would go. "Now are you going to be up here with me or down there with them?" he asked me.

I looked at him and laughed and said, "I'm no better than anybody else. I'm not up there and I certainly ain't down there. I am just where

I am intended to be." I didn't fall for the same trick again. It was the same thing Larry had tried to do – by taking away all my family and friends, Andy thought he was being clever about controlling me. I couldn't believe what I had just heard. Eventually, I walked away from that relationship with exactly what I needed: some self-confidence, my son, and another example of what I didn't want in a relationship. I didn't need to be someone's charity case. I just needed to be cared about and loved for who I was.

CHAPTER 9

LABELING AND BALANCING YOUR STORY

"It is the nature of the self to manifest itself. In every atom slumbers the might of the self." [Muhammad Igbal]

By this point in my story, you are likely observing a trend in my life which I also began to recognize at this time. That is, I seem to always fall for the "wrong" kind of men. I have spent a long time judging myself for my choices in men, especially after it became clear that I never seemed to find the kind of man I needed, and was always attracted to the ones who treated me badly.

I have come to understand that none of the "wrong" men in my life were really all that wrong, because each of them gave me something I needed (and a lot of things I didn't!). There was something I needed in my life's path that was provided each and every time I fell for the "wrong" man. They were all supposed to be on my path to help me move a little farther along it, and that is never "wrong".

In the past I have struggled with looking at my life objectively though, especially with the mistakes I have made, and feeling sorry for myself because I have been what some might consider a victim. It wasn't until recently I got the answer to this question I sent out to the Universe: How do I give advice or show people how to change their perspective about life to manifest what they want when, at times, I can't always feel good about my own life? Don't get me wrong, I still get sad, I don't always have a good perspective, I feel sorry for myself and I even feel anger and guilt. But I received an answer on how to change my perspective on life to manifest what I want (healthy, forward-looking perspective), not what I don't want (looking in reverse, with feelings of anger and guilt). Amazingly the answer came to me through a conversation I had with a new friend and he just happens to be a preacher. Of all the people in all the world it was surprisingly a preacher who explained it to me, but he didn't even realize what his words meant to me.

The reverend and I had been having an in depth conversation about life. In the course of conversation and getting to know one another, we agreed we are both advice givers, although we go about it in different ways. The reverend said to me, "I am two different people. I am a preacher and I am a man." His words went on, but I had what I needed from that conversation; those few words were so precious to me, he had answered my dilemma. It wasn't that I didn't already know all this about myself, but it was as if the preacher gave me permission to be okay with playing two different roles, almost like having two personalities.

The preacher was speaking about the two parts of his human energy. His explanation is what gave me clarification that we all have many different levels of who we are. There is the version of me who is here to be a physical human being, or conscious; there is my subconscious, the part that stores everything and uses it to protect me; and there is the superconscious, or my higher self. It is the part of me that can say, "Everything happens for a reason," and it is the part of me that has access to the whole. This part takes the human emotion or feelings out of the equation so that I can be objective, and it is this part that looks at life as just an experience, not something that is right or wrong.

It is important to understand when I talk about having a different point of view that this doesn't mean you can't still have other point of views and see another perspective. It just means we must pay attention to which set of eyes we are looking through in any given circumstance.

It's okay to be human and make mistakes, its okay if your subconscious creates something you didn't want, and it is okay to know and believe in your higher self. They all make up your experience and the sooner you can get them working together, the better off and easier your life will be. Deciding to change your point of view might mean that you get to take a little part of each view to make one that suits you. They are all part of how you saw things, so there is not harm in picking and choosing the elements that serve you. The benefit is you become unique, made up of all three parts, a mixture that allows you to flow through life instead of struggling with it.

What happens if you have too much of one entity and not enough of the others? Or maybe you are all human, a little subconscious and are in tune with very little of your higher self. This results in imbalance, where you are living as someone you are not. Understanding and accepting all three entities are there and communicating between those entities strengthens the ties that bind them, and keeps your perspective in balance and harmonious with your true self.

What happens if those ties are weak, or how would a person know they are weak? Things become unstable. Look to nature for proof of this – we can see examples of instability everywhere, in ecology, weather and life cycles, for example. When thinking about what makes each of your entities special and how we can tell the difference between them, it really depends on what your thoughts, emotion and beliefs are of your human self, subconscious self and higher self. To know where to look in nature, I often ask myself this question: tangibly, what are thoughts, emotions or beliefs made of? If I had to describe them I would say they are made up of space, including positive, neutral and/ or negative energy, similar to an atom.

What is an atom made of? Think back to your junior high school science days and recall that the parts of an atom (you) are called +protons (human self), -electron (subconscious) and the neutron (higher self). When you change any of these parts by adding or taking away, you change the element (your reality) which are made up of the atoms. When the binding between the protons, electron and neutron is weak, the atom becomes unstable and makes an unstable element. This is all going on inside the atom and this is all going on inside you. The labels we put on these particles are, protons have a positive charge; electrons have a negative charge; and neutrons which have no charge, they are neutral.

The important word in the information I just gave you was the word 'label'. The word label is important because positive, negative and neutral are subjective terms. You have to have all those particles in different amounts to make up our elements and if we didn't, everything and every experience would be the same. This would never allow all things to happen. So you have permission to be depressed or happy and it is fine to love or hate, these are all just subjective terms we use to label and make sense of what is in our world.

It is important to have a rational, practical amount of the protons, neutrons and electrons. It doesn't have to be too balanced, but somewhere in the range of balanced. Without one part to keep the others in check, the perspectives become distorted or toxic. In the middle of the atom is a nucleus made up of the protons and neutrons. They huddle together kind of like the heart of the atom. Electrons are like a guard keeping watch. They strategically make their rounds, watching the nucleus and keeping it in its place at the heart. If that nucleus becomes too big and the electron disappears, how does a positive now know it is positive? How does a proton know what its purpose is? Neutrons don't care either way what it is, it doesn't have an opinion. When a proton sees a neutron, it's like looking in the mirror, it sees a positive. Without enough electrons there is nothing opposite for a proton to reflect itself off of. It would just keep growing and growing and then the atom starts to try to get rid of all this energy. It just can't all be contained in that one atom. Trying to expel all these extra particles is what we call radiation.

You know what I am talking about if you have ever been around a person who makes you sick because of their annoyingly constant positive attitude. Do not get me wrong, a positive attitude is important, but what these people are doing is spewing so much positive on others it is creating an adverse effect causing more vibrational negative radiation in other people. They think by being positive with everyone all the time they will attract only positive situations to themselves. People can only take so much before it becomes positively draining and they want to tell these people to shut the hell up. It is something I can personally only take in small doses. It is because I am so sensitive to the vibrations in the universe, and you probably are too.

I have the same problem with people who are too negative. I can only be around certain people for short periods of times before I actually will start to get physically sick. I want to encourage them and help them, but the amount of positive it takes to do that is a hardship on me physically and mentally. It is nature's way of trying to always balance things out so we don't end up with toxic waste all over the place. Nature's propensity for trying to maintain balance is another reason why we have this observation about human nature that says, when someone wants you to do something, you generally want to do the exact opposite.

There is a lot more we could discuss in terms of learning about ourselves in the context of this science lesson. For example, we could talk about how, almost always, protons have the same exact number of neutrons, and how they can even be broken down further to quarks. Or I could explain how electrons are elementary particles and can't be split and they are so much smaller then protons. I could tell you what all this means related to how you attract things to yourself, but that is not my mission here. I am just supposed to only explain that you are okay in your story and if you want it better, embrace those positive and negative things in life and about yourself. Open the lines of communication between your different selves to make the element, known as you, stronger. You get to decide and put the label on things in your world.

All of this comes down to taking responsibility for creating what is going on in your world, and knowing that what you create and include in your world is a conscious choice. The human or conscious part of me knows that there are people out there in the world who may read what I write and not completely understand or believe in total responsibility and that you have contracts and bring everything to you. I have actually run into this sort of behavior a lot lately. I have realized those that are rejecting my ideas of how things are do so because there is something I have not yet come to terms with about the concept. In order for me to be able to move forward to help you better, I must address these issues. I have come to the conclusion it is an issue of acceptance. I accept that each person opposing my beliefs and challenging them are all parts of me, challenging my new beliefs. How does that work with someone reading my book and helping them? It works like this: you have created this book to challenge your old beliefs and to give you new ideas, or you have created it to confirm how strongly you feel about your beliefs. I am learning patience as everyone is just on their own path to their own place with their own experience, and what exists for them is true and real in their world.

Allowing the experience to happen doesn't mean you can't interfere by lending a hand, such as by giving money to a homeless woman and her children. It is their experience and, yes, they are going to have it no matter what you do, but you have written them into your contact right at that moment and you are a part of theirs. How do you know when and where you are needed, especially since there are so many people in this world that need help? They will come across your path; one way or another they will find you. When they show up, you will know because it is that feeling you get when you see someone you just know you have to help and the hair stands up on the back of your neck, you get goose bumps or you just can't turn and walk away. I call this inspiration. Inspiration comes when the human self, subconscious and higher self are at complete perfect communication and working inside the exact terms of the contract. Inspiration is the energy created by you being at your absolute best and in absolute harmony and balance.

This is what has happens when I write. You give me inspiration to write what comes to my mind and I know when I'm on the right track because it feels like the angels are putting their hands on my back as I type the words of this or any of my books. It is divine and in that moment, I know I am doing what I am supposed to be doing. It isn't a struggle, it all just flows.

I know I make it sound so easy and there are times it is, but there are times when life in general is extremely hard and I don't feel like even getting out of bed. Do you feel this way too? If you do, you are who I am writing for. There are going to be people out there like me who have a bad day, week and year. Sometimes you don't even want to be happy or do things that are fun. When you have suffered so much and hurt so badly, it puts a blanket over the small little things that seem to make everyone else happy. Then there are going to people who are going to tell you how wrong you are to be negative and make you feel like you just aren't ever going to get it when it comes to law of attraction, conscious manifestation, and self-help. That stuff is great for the rest of the world, but we are different. We have been through hell and back and it takes a piece of something from us. You just have to know in yourself, somewhere deep inside, you are not a victim. And when you do, you won't find that piece of you that is missing because it is gone. That piece you're missing is your innocence, it won't ever come back. What you will find to take its place is strength and power.

It isn't more positivity that people who have had hardships need to focus on to manifest their desires. We have to do it differently; we have to find something bigger then ourselves to consciously manifest things. We have to see purpose in what we desire or it doesn't mean anything to us. When you have gone through life a victim, it is obvious what you know and believe about yourself, so then why would you create anything you want? You are deserving, but you don't know that.

You are worth having everything you want, but you don't know that. Does this statement feel true to you? "If I am not sacrificing then I am selfish." Until you can change that, you have to find something bigger then yourself to create for.

We can all work with what we have until we can come upon something that will help us change. This is manifestation for the rest of us. Our way of looking at life and how we feel isn't any worse or any better than how someone else does it, it is just different. When I wrote earlier about labels, that is all what you feel is. You define the labels for what you are feeling. Give yourself a break; don't try to fit in every self-help guru's shape of how to manifest and live a good life. That is what is good for them and those that need their information have found it. If you are like me, it all sounds good and makes sense, but it is a struggle. You are not alone because I was, and sometimes still am, right there with you trying to manifest what I want when I can't even remember what "good" feels like because the other feelings are so strong they consume everything around them. Love yourself and be patient with yourself, and remember that manifesting what you desire might take some time. Manifesting is a process and journey of its own, one in which there are no wish-granting genies or magic wands. But you'll get there, I know you will.

CHAPTER 10

REMEMBER YOUR CONTRACT

"The talent for being happy is appreciating and liking what you have, instead of what you don't have." [Woody Allen]

To get where you want to be you have to do something important. This something is important, significant, but simple. That is, remember. Remember your contract. If you are going through something or have gone through something so bad you are a victim, remember why you had to go through it. What is its purpose? It isn't to make you feel sad or to feel like you have been hurt. Those are just nasty side effects to help you learn you lessons faster. Look back at what you have gone through and see what it was for. Who are you now because of it? Chances are you are now, or by the time you are done you will be, a helper!

Helpers are those who figure things out about life by experiencing difficult things for the rest of us, then they share what they know with others, either through being a social worker, counselor, alternative healer, artist or any of the other helping professions. You are not destined to do this with your life, but helping others in life is what will make you happy.

Sit in any college class of psychology students for an hour and you will find almost all their personal stories will be full of hardships and hurt, but there is also something special about these people. That special something is a passion for preventing the bad or having compassion for and helping others just like them.

Even without being a helper you are so important in this world, it can't be what it is without you. Even if you are miserable, you are contributing to what this world is as a whole. Without you there is something missing. Notice what you have given yourself to keep you here and to keep going. Only you can answer that question. If you are depressed, lost, and don't want to be in this world, it is alright to feel that way if you remember that feeling will pass. There are ways to tap into that higher self once in a while and look at things objectively, even if just for a few minutes.

The best examples I have of looking at my life objectively come from when have made the time to sit down and write my stories. I have had this habit of jotting down my thoughts and things that have happened for many years. This is how I am able to give you my ideas. In the previous books I have written, I go through parts of my contract and I am going to do it again. I won't explain it all in detail, instead I will focus on what is important. I will do this so you understand what it looks like when you are looking at your life objectively and this helps with the process of figuring out your life contract for yourself. How my sister Cindy treated me, Larry's abuse and the experience with Andy are examples of them doing what they needed to fulfill their obligation to me. They all taught me too many lessons to count, like how resilient I am. You can knock me down, but I keep getting back up. I was taught how to find my priority, which is usually something that means more to me than me. It may not be a completely right or logical point of view, but it is mine.

There has been nothing logical about my life and it seems I have a knack for doing things the hard way. The more difficult the events of my life were, the more meaning they have to me and the more I cherish them. It isn't always the bad stuff that I cherish because the good times mean something too. However it is the hardships that I have learned the most from. Anything that helped me through those times are the things I cling to when I need to get through life. When I developed my phobia of driving my counselor showed me something about myself I didn't know and this might just be one of the most important words of advice I have gotten in my life. She said, "You look too far down the road."

What this meant to me then and now is, I always try to analyze life and everything around me. I try to think of every possibility so I can be prepared. A lot of times there is no need to think so far ahead. It is good to be prepared, but when it stops you from living then it is wrong. I learned to stop looking so far ahead. Sometimes I just need to make it to the next stop sign or the next one mile, or sometimes it means just getting through the next 5 minutes of life. When everything feels chaotic and the world is coming to an end, I try to remember not to look so far down the road.

It is a good thing to not look too long or too hard at the road behind you either. For me it is alright to look back in recognition and observance of the past, but I try not to stay there too long. The human mind wants to dwell there and not be objective about all the things that have happened. The subconscious likes to keep the past to help protect me by replaying things over and over.

The human and subconscious parts of me find it hard to write this next part. I know this isn't going to be a popular way of thinking and you might not even like me for saying this, but I am compelled to. It is the people in our lives that have made it tough, miserable or down right unbearable for us to live who deserve the biggest thank you. It would be the easy thing in life to be a well-liked, lovable person never causing anyone grief or heartache. People like my sister and like Larry go through their own pain and agony. They live in their own suffering to be who they need to be to help us along our path. If they didn't sacrifice being a popular person, we would not get our little lessons in life. With each and every thing my sister and Larry taught me about life and myself, it made the impact of the important lessons bearable.

I know being aware that there are other stories worse than yours and mine doesn't mean much or make you feel better, and that's okay. The way you feel is just fine, and your personal story is the most important one.

I haven't talked to my sister for years and Larry is long gone and out of my life. At first when the wounds were fresh and I hurt so bad from all they had done to me, I hated them. It was hard to just sit back and not take revenge, but I was so scared of both of them the fear paralyzed me. The fear was a good thing though because I didn't do take action to fill my need for revenge, and they ruined themselves all on their own anyway, without me. I learned to move on and to stop being their victim by seeing the value they had in my world and to the whole. I don't have to be a mean person, because they are doing it for me. I don't have to be an abuser, because they are. I know more about who I am as an individual because of what they put me through. It is hard to remember I created all of it, but I did and it all happened for a reason. I do take credit for all the lessons I have given myself. They were all in the contract I created for myself, and I regularly do the simple, important thing I asked you to do at the beginning of this chapter: remember your contract.

I have learned I am also a person who needs to be sad sometimes. Sometimes my sadness is even a little comforting, like I have gone to my metaphysical home. Sad is a safe place, it means I am already in a place where I can't be hurt. Sad is familiar and as you know, if you are around long enough the seasons will change. That is how I feel about sadness. It's a season. I am not trying to be depressing, I promise. My motive in explaining my relationship with sadness is about positivity. This is how I manifest from my sadness. Remember when I said it was about labels? You can label your feelings as depression or sadness, but the point of view and the meaning behind it is what is important.

If you think your sadness is warm, if you think loneliness is bliss, then that is what is important. Even if you don't agree with what's going on around you or feel good about your feelings, it is helpful if you can accept that you have them and that it is okay if you do. Your feelings about your life are what you are manifesting from, not your labels. Manifest from a place where your point of view is different and you will manifest the things you desire. Manifest by finding something to manifest which means more to you than, you and you will always manifest the important things.

My own manifestations might have seemed like a series of bad events in my life and back then, that is all they were to me. I was always looking for that feeling of home I had lost when mom died, always looking for a man who could love me unconditionally like my father should have. I was always searching for something better than what I had, never feeling like I belonged to this world. I always felt like everything I did was going to be wrong. I questioned myself daily – would I ever get the hang of this life thing like everyone else seemed to? I still have these feelings and ideas, but now I know why.

Wondering why you can't be like everyone else creates demons and monsters inside you that someday will break their way out to the real world and wreak havoc on your life. If you run and hide, your fears will not be ignored and eventually you will be standing face-to-face with them. Find your nerve to step into your nightmare and yell in its face. You can do it because you would never give yourself anything you can't handle. Fear will make you bitter, but it is only when your worst fears come true that you get to see how strong you really are.

I just couldn't figure out how the heck everyone else could be so happy when I was so sad. Being around Russell and having my children close to me would make me happy, but as soon as they weren't around me I was sad again. This is the problem a lot of people have – they look for everything outside of themselves to make them whole. They grasp at anything to hold onto in order to make themselves happy. Their self-talk sounds like this: "If I could only have a different job, I'd be happy," or, "If only I could get that certain person to love me and be with me, I'd be happy." "If only my kids would listen, I would be happy." Then when you acquire what you wanted and the relationship or situation doesn't make you happy, you blame that person or thing for your unhappiness and you began to despise the very thing you had wanted so badly. I struggle with this very issue myself.

This is all backwards and I know it because I live it. We should only worry about how our hearts can be full, even when there is nothing else in our world. Nothing outside yourself didn't start in your mind and your heart first. To fix that emptiness and sadness on the outside you have to fix the emptiness and sadness inside you first.

Being a creature of habit I aimed for the utopia of making Russell and the kids the focus of my happiness. Russell and I grew closer and closer, and two best friends soon became more. It seemed natural to add intimacy to our relationship and being around him felt safe and right, even if no one thought it was. People in our lives thought our age difference was odd and didn't understand why a woman would want a man who is seven years younger than her. I say the heart wants what the heart wants and there was a matter of destiny or something in our contract we needed to fulfill.

Russell and the kids and I started living together and we were becoming a real family. Even though we were careful, I got pregnant, but I was happy about it. This time I wasn't as sick as I had been in my other pregnancies. Russell worked his butt off so I could stay home and take care of Grif and be there for Haley and Alex. He never made me feel guilty for being a stay-at-home mom. He was happy for me. It was a nice balance of what I wanted. I could come and go as I please, and I could stay home and be there for my kids. Russell never made me feel trapped like Larry or my sister had, and he was nothing like the dictator Andy had been. He never made me feel like I owed him anything for the privilege of being a stay-at-home mom. He was young, but responsible and we were best friends. We were family.

We didn't have a lot of money, but we were living life the best we could. Haley was eleven by that point, Alex was eight. Haley started to rebel and this was the first time I realized I had no idea how to raise a teenager. Mom died when I was just eleven so I had no reference as to what a mother and teenage daughter relationship should look like. I was in uncharted territory.

Even though I was unsure about what I was doing with Haley, I stuck to my one true purpose: be a mom. That was the only purpose I wanted to have at the time. I woke up every morning knowing this was my life and I was okay with the idea. It was boring, but I was content. To me being content means I was just sad enough for it to matter, but happy enough to continue on every day. I always felt like there was more to life and that I was missing something, but I figured I would do that when the kids all grew up. I guess that is what kept me going most of the time, the never ending feeling there was something else out there I was supposed to be doing.

Despite whatever wrongs there were in the world, I was in love and I had my whole life ahead of me. For once in my life I was as close to happiness as I could be or have ever been. I went to bed at night knowing I was going to without a doubt get up the next day and I started to find comfort in that. I knew I was going to get my kids up out of bed and we would get ready for school and I could do whatever I wanted to during the day and I could do it while taking care of Grif. I knew day after day the balance was shifting and there was more laughter in one day than there would be sadness.

Little did I know I had some underlining beliefs that just weren't in alignment with the belief that I was allowed to be happy, safe and comfortable. The last time I had come close to those feelings when I was a little girl, everything got ripped away from me the moment my mother died. I was conditioned to know if life becomes too happy and good, then it was all about to be taken away. It was out of my control. I didn't know it at the time, but the universe was just about to prove me right again. My own happiness, comfort, safety will be my own downfall as I had not done the work to transform the beliefs I had picked up throughout my life. It wasn't time for me to transform those beliefs just yet; there was one more important thing I needed to do before I would learn that everything really does happen for a reason.

EPILOGUE

This is what I have to give to the world and to you, not as advice per se, but simply as words that come from my own experience. You will probably never decide the time is right to get out of an abusive relationship. However, when it is time, you will know. Something has to push you to leave. Of course it will be obvious to everyone around you long before you come to the point that you know it is time to go, and there will be many people who will try to fix everything for you. You will feel the need to reject their ideas, suggestions and pressure to leave. Keep an open mind and know they only want to help. You never know when just one thoughtful idea might help.

I have thought about words of advice I can give someone who is in an abusive relationship. Then I think about what would have helped me. There were never any words that could have pushed me far enough to leave. The best thing that anyone did for me was nothing! That's exactly what I am going to do for you. I could direct you towards a hundred different websites. I could list a hundred numbers to different woman shelters. I am not going to do those things because, again, from my experience, I know they are not what will help you.

You are smart and have gotten yourself through the battle this far. If you want to know where shelters and websites are, you are intelligent enough to know where to find this information. Your intuition will know how your story will play out and you are on the right path to discovering when your time is right. There is no instruction manual about surviving abuse and I will not take away from your story or journey by trying to give you something you don't want or need. You are the creator and the knowledge and ideas you have acquired from my books was created by you, so use it.

Know there are bigger things to come for you and me. You are not the sum of the equation. You are much more then what you see. You are going to contribute what you have gone through and no one can do it, no one but you. What you need to hear is take it day by day and make it to the next day; and trust that when the time is right, you will know. As much as I know now that my story was leading me to something special, I know your story will lead you to a purpose too. I am here to motivate and inspire you to hang in there and get to your destination. My story is just beginning and I hope you know yours is too.

Maybe the person reading this is someone watching a loved one being abused. It is a time for you to learn to allow. Allow your loved one to find their own way. Allow yourself to be there when needed. Don't be disappointed if the abused person in your life never takes your advice. Everything happens in its own time and in its own way. This is just as much about you as it is about them. Step in when you need to, but know it has to be their ideas that get them through the storm. When the lessons are learned, they will know.

A journey is a person in itself; no two are alike. And all plans, safeguards, policing, and coercion are fruitless. We find that after years of struggle that we do not take a trip; a trip takes us. [John Steinbeck]

www.ingramcontent.com/pod-product-compliance
Lightning Source LLC
Chambersburg PA
CBHW061746020426

42331CB00006B/1374